BWB Texts

Short books on big subjects from
great New Zealand writers

Safeguarding the Future

Governing in an Uncertain World

JONATHAN BOSTON

Published in 2017 by Bridget Williams Books Limited, PO Box 12474, Wellington 6144, New Zealand, www.bwb.co.nz, info@bwb.co.nz

ISBN 9780947518257 (Paperback), ISBN 9780947518264 (EPUB)
ISBN 9780947518271 (KINDLE), ISBN 9780947518288 (PDF)
DOI 10.7810/9780947518257

A catalogue record for this book is available from the National Library of New Zealand. Kei te pātenga raraunga o Te Puna Mātauranga o Aotearoa te whakarārangi o tēnei pukapuka

Acknowledgements
The publisher acknowledges the ongoing support provided by the Bridget Williams Books Publishing Trust and Creative New Zealand.

Publisher: Tom Rennie
Editor: Anna Hodge
Cover and internal design: Base Two
Typesetter: Tina Delceg
Printer: Printlink, Wellington

CONTENTS

1. ANTICIPATING AND SAFEGUARDING THE FUTURE

We know that we are stewards of a precious 'pale blue dot' in a vast cosmos with a future measured in billions of years. But despite these vastly expanded conceptual horizons, politics and economics are short-term and parochial.

– Lord Martin Rees[1]

This little book is about anticipating and safeguarding the future. More specifically, it is about how democratic societies, in the face of powerful political pressures to prioritise short-term goals, can better protect the long-term interests of their current and future citizens. How, in other words, can the quality of 'intergenerational governance'[2] and 'anticipatory governance'[3] be improved? While this book focuses on Aotearoa New Zealand, the arguments advanced and the reforms proposed have much wider applicability. Potentially they are relevant to governments everywhere, certainly all democratic ones.

The challenge of protecting the interests of future generations has many dimensions and the problem can be posed in multiple ways.[4] For many people the issue is simple, immediate and personal: it is about ensuring that their children, grandchildren and all subsequent offspring inherit a society and world that is hospitable, safe, healthy and sustainable. It is about the steps that must be taken – whether locally, nationally or globally – to best safeguard their future. For others, especially those of a more philosophical disposition, the problem concerns the nature and demands of intergenerational justice.[5] What ethical principles should guide how benefits and burdens are shared between people over extended periods of time – including multiple generations? And how should such principles be applied, not only within nation states but also globally? Alternatively, the challenge can be framed in terms of societal welfare or wellbeing. In the words of the distinguished New Zealand economist Girol Karacaoglu, the challenge is how to ensure 'collective intergenerational wellbeing'.[6] Many other conceptualisations are also possible. For Pope Francis the task is to encourage wise stewardship and realise the 'long-term common good',[7] while for others the goal is to protect the 'long-term public interest' or achieve 'sustainable development'.

But however the long-term goal is framed and regardless of the ethical principles that are deemed relevant to the quest, many practical questions arise. Some of these are political, others are policy-oriented. How, for instance, can democratic institutions, policy-making processes and analytical frameworks be designed in ways that increase the likelihood of long-term interests receiving adequate attention? How can elected officials be equipped and incentivised to protect the interests not only of citizens today but also the citizens of tomorrow? How, in other words, can the chances of short-sighted policy decisions – ones that threaten or undermine citizens' long-term wellbeing – be minimised? Questions of this nature are the focus of this book. As such, therefore, the approach here is more practical than ethical and more applied than conceptual: it is about designing political institutions and policy processes to improve long-term societal outcomes.

Sceptical readers may already be contemplating numerous objections. What, for instance, constitutes a *short-sighted* decision? To what extent, especially in a complex and uncertain world, is it possible for governments to *anticipate*, let alone *safeguard*, the future? Is it really feasible in democracies – with short electoral cycles, impatient voters, populist movements, fake news and powerful vested interests – to shift the political fulcrum more in favour of future interests? Surely, in a world of Brexit, Donald Trump, post-truth politics, religious extremism, massive inequality, growing corruption and mounting ecological crises, such suggestions are utopian and far-fetched. Surely they are unrealistic politically. These objections are perfectly understandable. They deserve answers. That is the purpose of the pages which follow.

THE VIRTUE OF ANTICIPATION

Anticipation – in the sense of alertness, prepared-ess, readiness, watchfulness and vigilance – is a vital human trait. Without it we would constantly falter and fail. We all anticipate the future, albeit to varying degrees. And on the basis of what we expect – whether good or bad – we take action. We respond proactively, avoiding possible dangers and seizing new opportunities. As we approach a sharp bend on a narrow road, we think about whether a car might be coming in the opposite direction and, if so, whether there will be room to pass. In assessing the risks, we may slow down, hover our foot over the brake pedal and steer closer to the curb. In our journey through school or a tertiary institution, we ponder what jobs might be of interest and what subjects must be taken to secure the requisite skills and qualifications. And we may adjust the courses we take to increase our prospects of future employment. As we grow older, we consider our retirement and assess, amongst other things, whether our projected income will cover our likely expenses. If we have concerns, we may save harder or reduce our expected costs, for instance by buying a smaller car or cheaper home.

People differ, of course, in the extent to which they anticipate the future: some are active planners or strategic thinkers, while others are not. People also vary in their capacity to assess risks, as well as their willingness to take them: some are overly cautious, while others can be reckless or foolhardy. But whatever our personalities, aptitudes or appetite for risk, the capacity to anticipate – to think ahead, to look forward, to exercise foresight, to contemplate possible problems and consider alternative scenarios and solutions – is essential for living well. If we fail to anticipate what lies ahead or if we fail to be proactive, we are bound to stumble and bungle. We will also miss important, rewarding and productive opportunities. Hence, for individuals, a failure to anticipate is incompatible with wise stewardship or long-term wellbeing.

The same applies at the collective level – whether for organisations, corporations or governments. Sound anticipatory processes are essential for good governance – and good long-term results. Governments cannot govern their societies well if they lack proper foresight. To protect future interests – whether of current or future citizens – policy-makers must look ahead, strategise, plan and prioritise. They must not only tackle the urgent challenges of today, they must also contemplate and respond to the problems of tomorrow. A failure to do so can result in significant costs, unpleasant surprises and missed opportunities. Accordingly, governments must assess the implications of current trends and be alert to looming issues. To do this well, they need good intelligence, robust evidence, and competent advice.

But good anticipatory governance entails something more: it requires a commitment to 'future-proofing' public institutions and protecting the long-term public interest.[8] This means taking a long view – looking well beyond the immediate horizon or the next election. It means giving proper attention to issues with long-term consequences, proactively identifying, mitigating and managing significant threats, wrestling with complex intertemporal trade-offs, and recognising the risk that pressing day-to-day demands can readily override more distant, but often far more weighty, concerns. Put succinctly, it means taking care of tomorrow today.

WHY ANTICIPATORY GOVERNANCE IS HARD

Yet good anticipatory governance does not come easily. Governments face formidable hurdles: powerful lobby groups, populist pressures, scarce resources, limited information, competing priorities, difficult policy trade-offs and short electoral cycles. Two problems deserve particular mention at this juncture: first, the ever-present phenomenon of uncertainty, including the fact that some of the events we encounter are not only unfamiliar and unexpected, but also unimaginable prior to them happening; and second, a presentist bias in policy-making (i.e. an undue focus on short-term interests at the expense of long-term interests).

Uncertainty

Plainly, the future is characterised by uncertainty. We cannot be *absolutely* sure what will happen over the coming weeks, months or years. And the further our time horizons are extended, the deeper the uncertainty we encounter. Significant, surprising events – or what Nassim Taleb calls 'black swans' – are inevitable.[9] Such events lie beyond the realm of normal expectations. There are many examples. For large numbers of people, the referendum decision in June 2016 for Britain to leave the European Union and the subsequent victory of Donald Trump in the American presidential elections came as great surprises, if not rude shocks. Closer to home, John Key's resignation as Prime Minister on 5 December 2016 took political observers and citizens by complete surprise.

To complicate matters, governments face not only the 'known unknowns' – such as when the next major earthquake, drought, flood or financial crisis might strike – but also the 'unknown unknowns – the ones we don't know we don't know', as Donald Rumsfeld, a former American Secretary of Defense, famously put it.[10] There are many things, in other words, that cannot readily be anticipated or even imagined. Many people find this troubling. But it is an integral part of the world we inhabit. As the French philosopher Voltaire once observed, 'Uncertainty is an uncomfortable position. But certainty is an absurd one.'

There are, of course, different levels of uncertainty. At one end of the spectrum are situations where we have a high level of confidence, albeit not absolute certainty: the sun, we trust, will continue to shine. At the other end we encounter the phenomenon known as *deep* uncertainty.[11] According to Robert Lempert, Steven Popper and Steven Bankes at the RAND Corporation, deep uncertainty can be defined as:

the condition in which analysts do not know or the parties to a decision cannot agree upon (1) the appropriate models to describe interactions among a system's variables, (2) the probability distributions to represent uncertainty about key parameters in the models, and/or (3) how to value the desirability of alternative outcomes.[12]

In other words, deep uncertainty occurs when causality is poorly understood, when probabilities cannot be assigned and there is much controversy over the ranking of different policy goals. Deep uncertainty arises in many policy contexts and can render traditional analytical tools and techniques inappropriate or of little value. Anthropogenic climate change provides a good example: while there is much we know, there is also much uncertainty – for instance, about the various tipping points in the climate system, the likely speed and magnitude of sea level rise, and the costs and benefits of different mitigation strategies.

In short, the quest for sound anticipatory governance must reckon squarely with uncertainty – in all its forms. It must be built, therefore, on the twin foundations of realism and humility. There are fundamental limits to what human beings can reasonably foresee or predict. No amount of forecasting, imagining, speculating or contemplation can overcome such limitations. Surprises – sometimes dramatic and shocking ones – are unavoidable. Yet while we must be prepared to be surprised, one of the goals of anticipatory governance must be to minimise the frequency with which we are surprised by events and outcomes which should have come as no surprise. Another goal must be to enhance the capacity of our governmental institutions to cope with surprises. This entails greater resilience.

A presentist bias

A second major challenge to good anticipatory governance is the tendency for governments to give excessive weight to short-term interests and considerations, thereby putting future interests at risk. This tendency is variously referred to as short-termism, political myopia, policy short-sightedness, a present bias and a presentist bias.[13] Such a tendency is evident within multiple policy domains and across all levels and types of government. The widespread nature of this phenomenon suggests that it constitutes a general *disorder*. In other words, it represents a systemic governance problem, not simply a policy problem or a problem specific to a particular policy domain. As such, it cannot be ameliorated merely by changes to discrete policy settings. It requires a more holistic and comprehensive response.

As to the causes of the presentist bias, there are many. These will be discussed more fully in Chapter 2. For now it is enough to mention that one of them is the tendency for people to discount the future while another is due to uncertainty. As a broad generalisation, the more uncertain we are about possible future costs or benefits, the less weight we tend to place on them. Hence, as uncertainty increases, there is a heightened risk that our time horizons will shrink.

The presentist bias is reflected in the propensity for governments to prefer policies that front-load the benefits – whether for citizens, taxpayers or important sectors – and back-load the costs (i.e., to shift the costs beyond a politically significant event, such as the next election, or perhaps onto future generations). Similarly, it is indicated in governments favouring policy measures which minimise the upfront costs even though this will probably reduce overall societal payoffs.[14] Other examples include: failing to exercise proper foresight – for instance, by ignoring 'creeping' problems and those which have a cumulative or snowballing dimension (see Chapter 2); downplaying certain kinds of risk, including systemic risks; delaying measures to mitigate and manage well-established risks; and retaining policies that are demonstrably unsustainable, whether economically, socially or environmentally.

In New Zealand there have been many instances over the years of governments – both at the national and sub-national levels – favouring short-term interests, and especially their near-term electoral interests, at the expense of the long-term public interest. Amongst these are:

1. delays in adjusting the policy parameters of the New Zealand Superannuation Scheme in order to mitigate the long-term fiscal impacts of population ageing (e.g. by slowly raising the age of entitlement and/or adjusting the level of benefits);[15]

2. significant underinvestment in certain types of long-term public infrastructure and a failure, over many decades, to maintain the quality of the social housing stock;[16]

3. lengthy delays in implementing effective policies to reduce major environmental externalities, such as greenhouse gas emissions and the pollution of freshwater resources;[17]

4. a reluctance to invest in preventative or corrective measures of various kinds, notwithstanding reliable evidence of positive paybacks (or rates of return) on such investments (e.g. cost-effective measures to alleviate obesity, upgrade the quality of housing, reintegrate prisoners into the community, and reduce the scale and duration of child poverty);[18]

5. an unwillingness to support urban densification in the face of 'nimbyism' (i.e., a mentality of 'not in my back yard') by local communities;[19]

6. a reluctance to impose motorway tolls and congestion charges to ameliorate traffic congestion;[20]
7. a failure to impose efficient natural resources rents or save some of the proceeds from the exploitation of renewable and non-renewable resources for the benefit of future generations (e.g. via a sovereign wealth fund);[21] and
8. a propensity for political parties in the run-up to elections to make promises that, although electorally attractive, are questionable in terms of their intergenerational and intragenerational impacts (e.g. the Labour government's pre-election promise in 2005 to remove interest on student loans).

This is not to imply that near-term electoral imperatives are the only reason for governmental decisions that short-change the future. Likewise, it should not be assumed that there is an optimal – or uniquely correct – balance between competing intertemporal interests. Reasonable people might disagree, for instance, about the proper level and mix of societal investments for the future, including the extent to which it is justified to impose burdens on current generations in order to protect the interests of future generations. But this does not imply the absence of morally relevant criteria for assessing the desirability of policy decisions where significant intertemporal trade-offs are at stake. A core objective must be to avoid long-term outcomes that most people would regard as unacceptable (i.e., a no-regrets approach). For example, there is no justification for governments implementing measures that are likely to cause serious, widespread and irreversible harm. Nor are they justified in failing to manage and mitigate significant risks, including high-impact yet low-probability risks. As the martyred theologian Dietrich Bonhoeffer once claimed: 'the ultimate test of a moral society is the kind of world that it leaves to its children'. Parents generally strive to ensure that their children enjoy a better life than they themselves experienced. Governments should have the same ambition for their citizens. A better world, not a worse one, should be the goal.

While it is reasonable to assume that there is a presentist bias in policy-making in the democratic world, it does not follow that such tendencies are all-pervasive, constant, unrelenting or immutable. Nor is there any suggestion that politicians – or those they represent – are hopelessly or irredeemably myopic. On the contrary, there is evidence that short-termist policy-making varies over time, between governments and across policy domains. Indeed, there are numerous examples, both in New Zealand and elsewhere, of governments acting prudently to minimise future costs, taking precautionary measures to mitigate long-term risks, and drawing on the best available evidence to determine where to invest to maximise future societal returns.

Nevertheless, the evidence of a presentist bias in governmental decision-making is sufficiently strong that it would be unwise to ignore it. Moreover, changing societal expectations, cultural norms and technologies (e.g. the internet and social media) may be increasing its strength and prevalence. For one thing, there appears to be a growing mismatch between the time required to tackle complex social ills and the imperatives of electoral politics. For another, politicians in advanced democracies are under intensified pressures as a result of the 24-hour media cycle, coupled with public expectations for them to respond almost instantly to events.[22] To quote from a speech by former Prime Minister John Key:

Events can escalate quickly during a relentless 24 hour media cycle, now super-charged by social media .... social media eats your attention span .... it has also truncated our thinking time. 'It puts a premium on an immediate response, on tasks and information, but not on reflection.' ... One of the most valuable things that officials can do is filter out some of this noise and pressure, and help ministers focus on longer term considerations.[23]

But even if the presentist bias has not worsened, the potential for short-sighted policy decisions to generate damaging consequences undoubtedly has. Rapid technological advances, together with a massive increase in the global population and resource utilisation, mean that humanity has an ever-expanding capacity to cause harm – not only more severe and extensive harm, but also more persistent, if not irreversible, harm. For instance, in recent decades the scale and duration of human impacts on the environment have greatly increased.[24] Many leading scientists now believe that the epoch of the Holocene has ended and that a new geological epoch – the Anthropocene – has begun. This conclusion is based on evidence that human beings are now the largest driver of changes in the planet's biodiversity, biogeography, geomorphology and the climate system. In short, our ecological footprints have dramatically lengthened, widened and deepened. We now possess the capacity to destroy vast numbers of species and ecosystems, radically transform the Earth's climate, and impair critical life-support systems. If governments fail to acknowledge or anticipate such threats or are unwilling to prevent them because of short-term political pressures, then the long-term consequences for human wellbeing will be dire. Future generations will face incalculable losses. For many reasons, this matters.

Short-termist thinking and myopic policy-

making are not confined to democratic governments. In fact, non-democratic regimes almost
certainly perform even worse: their intertemporal
policy choices typically demonstrate even less
concern for the long-term interests of their
citizens and near neighbours. Nor is a presentist
bias restricted to the realm of politics. Far from
it. Short-termism appears to afflict most – if not
all – fields of human endeavour to one degree or
another, not least the world of business.[25] As Jo
Guldi and David Armitage argue:

almost every aspect of human life is plotted and judged,
packaged and paid for, on time-scales of a few months or
years. ... In the age of the permanent campaign, politicians
plan only as far as their next bid for election. They invoke
children and grandchildren in public speeches, but electoral
cycles of two to seven years determine which issues prevail.
The result is less money for crumbling infrastructure and
schools and more for any initiative that promises jobs
right now. The same short horizons govern the way most
corporate boards organise their futures. ... No one, it seems,
from bureaucrats to board members, or voters and recipients
of international aid, can escape the ever-present threat of
short-termism.[26]

But if escaping the presentist bias is not possible,
there is undoubtedly scope to mitigate its force and
counter its effects. Decision-makers – whether
corporate or governmental – have choices. They

are not at the mercy of some alien power. And their choices about intertemporal trade-offs are open to inspection and amenable to adjustment. Moreover, those in positions of political power can help shape the context in which such decisions are made. They can, if they so choose, endeavour to alter the decision-making environment – including its structures, rules, processes and incentives – in ways that shift the temporal focus towards the future, thereby better protecting long-term interests. For instance, they can establish countervailing mechanisms, such as future-focused institutions and various kinds of 'commitment devices',[27] to help alleviate myopic tendencies.

Arguably, such endeavours should be central to the task of wise stewardship and prudent anticipatory governance. Such governance, in other words, not only recognises the risks of short-changing the future because of short-termist pressures, but also actively develops political strategies, decision-making procedures and institutional mechanisms to reduce these risks. The purpose of this book is to identify and briefly assess such strategies, procedures and mechanisms, and then recommend a package of reforms to improve the quality of intergenerational governance in New Zealand.

In summary, good public governance must be future-oriented. It must be anticipatory. It must be alert to a wide range of risks, including the risk of a temporal bias towards the present. It must build public institutions that are forward-looking and future-focused – ones that take a long view and seek to protect long-term interests. The overall goal must be a better future – as judged on multiple criteria – for our children and all subsequent generations. Such a goal is fundamental to the implicit contract which binds humanity across multiple generations.[28] Moreover, it is consistent with the ethical values, principles and aspirations of most of the great religious and philosophical traditions which have informed the conduct of rulers and citizens over the course of human history.

ETHICAL ASSUMPTIONS

Two such ethical principles underpin the analysis which follows. To start with, all human beings are equally and intrinsically valuable. Their moral worth is equivalent irrespective of space and time. Hence, people born in 50 or 5,000 years from now are equally precious as those living today. There is no moral justification, therefore, in disadvantaging someone because of the timing of their birth. After all, people lack any control over when or where they are born – or, of course, to whom. Accordingly, as the philosopher John Rawls once argued, 'from a moral point of view, there are no grounds for discounting future wellbeing on the basis of pure time preference'.[29] Similarly, people ought to be impartially concerned for every period of their lives. To quote Rawls again: 'The mere difference of location in time, of something's being earlier or later, is not in itself a rational ground for having more or less regard for it.'[30]

The other fundamental assumption is that human beings have an abiding and non-negotiable moral duty to care for the Earth and everything that dwells within it. We are planetary stewards, environmental guardians and trustees of our cultural resources. As the American legal scholar Edith Brown Weiss argues:

The purpose of human society must be to realize and protect the welfare and well-being of every generation. This requires sustaining the life-support systems of the planet, the ecological processes, environmental conditions, and cultural resources important for the survival and well-being of the human species, and a healthy and decent human environment.[31]

In part, this duty of care rests on the fact that people enjoy significant capabilities, not least the gift of reason: we can anticipate the future, investigate risks, identify problems, imagine possibilities, contemplate options, calculate costs and benefits, and pursue solutions. Were such capabilities lacking, human beings would not be accountable for current or future outcomes.

THE STRUCTURE AND SCOPE OF THE BOOK

Chapter 2 highlights briefly the wide range of risks, both global and local, that contemporary governments must confront. As noted above, one of these is endogenous: it is the risk to good governance from within – namely the failure of policy-makers to exercise proper foresight and their tendency to yield unwisely to short-term pressures. In order to better understand the presentist bias in governmental decision-making, Chapter 2 discusses the types of policy problems where long-term interests are likely to be undervalued and thus most vulnerable. It also examines briefly some of the deeper causes of the presentist bias.

Following this, Chapter 3 explores in more detail the nature of anticipatory governance and outlines various criteria for assessing the quality of such governance. Having established some relevant benchmarks, Chapter 4 evaluates the quality of New Zealand's policy-making institutions and frameworks, reviews their performance as judged by recent policy outcomes, and considers the long-term implications of current outcomes.

Then, drawing on the relevant international literature, Chapter 5 proposes a package of reforms designed to mitigate the presentist bias and enhance the quality of anticipatory governance in New Zealand. Finally, Chapter 6 pulls the threads together and offers a few closing reflections.

The topics under discussion are large and complex. They cannot be fully investigated in a short study of this nature. Accordingly, the following analysis is partial and incomplete: it is an introductory text, not an advanced manual. Necessarily, many topics are omitted, including academic and policy debates surrounding:

1. concepts like sustainability, socio-ecological resilience and risk management;
2. various dimensions and forms of governance, such as adaptive governance, network governance and collaborative governance;
3. the nature and measurement of human needs, welfare and wellbeing; and
4. the nature of intergenerational justice.

Similarly, while this book is about safeguarding the future, it is not about futurology. It does not postulate possible, probable or preferable futures. Nor does it explore the grim consequences of humanity exceeding safe planetary boundaries or biophysical constraints, such as mass extinctions.[32] Likewise, this book says little about the profound economic or social implications of new and emerging technologies, such as artificial intelligence, advanced robotics, sentient tools, autonomous vehicles, 3D printing or the remarkable discoveries and inventions in the broad field of synthetic biology. Rather the purpose here is different: it is about enhancing anticipatory governance so that New Zealand is better able to adapt to, and cope with, the impacts of these technological innovations. Notable amongst such impacts will be major changes in the nature of work.[33]

Three other caveats warrant attention. First, while this book comments on governance arrangements in New Zealand at both the central and sub-national levels, the primary focus is on central government. Aside from limitations of space, this reflects the fact that New Zealand is a highly centralised unitary state, with the central government having responsibility for most of the important areas of public policy, such as health care, education, social services, taxation and transfer payments, including the regulation of private sector activities that are vital to risk management (e.g. the provision of telecommunications infrastructure).[34]

Second, the main focus in the following chapters is on *public* governance rather than the governance of private corporations or non-governmental organisations (NGOs). This is not to suggest that the governance of major corporates and NGOs is unimportant or that a presentist bias does not exist in these sectors.[35] On the contrary, there are solid grounds for taking action to counter short-termism, especially in business decision-making. But there is not the space to address such matters here.

Finally, the world is increasingly interdependent. In such a context, nation states have only a limited capacity to navigate their own course, let alone fully protect the future interests of their citizens. After all, many of the policy challenges facing governments are supranational: they extend far beyond the borders of individual nations. This includes protecting the planet's atmosphere, oceans and cyber-space. Effective solutions to global collective action problems require international cooperation. Accordingly, while sound anticipatory governance by nation states like New Zealand is necessary to protect the interests of future generations, it is not sufficient: good global governance – or Earth governance – is also required. Yet while acknowledging this, the scope of this analysis is modest. It deals with a single country – New Zealand.

CONCLUSION

Good governance requires robust anticipatory processes and institutions. To anticipate future problems and opportunities, governments need good intelligence. Equally, they must be mindful that not all risks can be foreseen; many will be unexpected, some even unimaginable. To govern well in the face of uncertainty, including deep uncertainty, governments need sound advice, especially about managing risk, nurturing societal resilience and enhancing adaptive capacity.

Amidst the unpredictable, policy-makers also confront several certainties. One of these is that some of the measures required for prudent long-term governance will be politically unattractive. In particular, near-term electoral concerns will sometimes be pitted against important long-term societal goals. In such circumstances there is an abiding risk that short-term considerations will prevail, thereby increasing the costs imposed on future generations. A presentist bias in policy-making is all the more troubling given humanity's ever-increasing capacity to inflict severe, widespread and persistent harm. The quest for sound anticipatory governance, therefore, must include the design and implementation of mechanisms to ameliorate this bias. The following chapters identify and assess such mechanisms, and recommend a package of effective reforms.

2. FAILING THE FUTURE
WHY GOVERNMENTS SHORT-CHANGE LONG-TERM INTERESTS

The future whispers while the present shouts.

– Al Gore[1]

Politicians are often unwilling to make investments that pay off only after they leave office.

– Ray Quay[2]

Governments face multiple risks. These include both exogenous and endogenous risks – those from without and those from within. A core responsibility of political leaders is to manage and mitigate both kinds of risks. To do so, such risks must be recognised, categorised and assessed. Despite numerous 'unknown unknowns', many of the risks confronting governments, both now and in the more distant future, can be readily identified: they are either 'known knowns' or 'known unknowns'. Such risks, of course, vary greatly in their likelihood and potential impacts.

To assist with the task of risk assessment, many international organisations, think tanks and businesses prepare regular, detailed risk analyses. One such example is the World Economic Forum, which publishes an annual report on global risks. This is based partly on an international survey of leaders from business, government, academia, civil society organisations and international organisations.[3]

Table 2.1 summarises thirty types of global risks, grouped into five categories: economic, environmental, geopolitical, societal and technological. The risks listed here represent those which were thought in late 2016 to pose the greatest threat over the coming decade. They exclude, of course, all those risks which are currently unknown.

The annual assessments undertaken by the World Economic Forum also identify the top five global risks, first by their likelihood, and second by their potential impact. The results, based on risk perception surveys conducted in 2014, 2015 and 2016, are outlined in Table 2.2.

Whatever the validity of such assessments, several matters are noteworthy. At least a third of the global risks rated amongst the top five during 2014–16 relate directly or indirectly to climate change (e.g. water crises, extreme weather events,

Table 2.1 Global risks as assessed by the World Economic Forum, 2016

Category of global risk	Type of global risk*
Economic	Asset bubble in a major economy
	Deflation in a major economy
	Failure of a major financial mechanism or institution
	Failure/shortfall of critical infrastructure
	Fiscal crisis in key economies
	High structural unemployment or underemployment
	Illicit trade (e.g. illicit financial flows, tax evasion, human trafficking, organised crime, etc.)
	Severe energy price shock (increase or decrease)
	Unmanageable inflation
Environmental	Extreme weather events (e.g. floods, storms, etc.)
	Failure of climate-change mitigation and adaptation
	Major biodiversity loss and ecosystem collapse (terrestrial or marine)
	Major natural disasters (e.g. earthquake, tsunami, volcanic eruption, geomagnetic storms)
	Man-made environmental damage and disasters (e.g. oil spills, radioactive contamination, etc.)
Geopolitical	Failure of national governance (e.g. failure of rule of law, corruption, political deadlock, etc.)
	Failure of regional or global governance
	Interstate conflict with regional consequences
	Large-scale terrorist attacks
	State collapse or crisis (e.g. civil conflict, military coup, failed states, etc.)
	Weapons of mass destruction
Societal	Failure of urban planning
	Food crises
	Large-scale involuntary migration
	Profound social instability
	Rapid and massive spread of infectious diseases
	Water crises
Technological	Adverse consequences of technological advances
	Breakdown of critical information infrastructure and networks
	Large-scale cyber attacks
	Massive incident of data fraud/theft

*A global risk is defined as an uncertain event or condition that, if it occurs, can cause significant negative impact for several countries or industries within the next decade.

Source: adapted from the World Economic Forum, *The Global Risks Report 2017*, 12th edition, Geneva, World Economic Forum, 2017, pp.61–64, based on a global risk perception survey conducted during September and early October 2016.

and the challenges of mitigation and adaptation). Another third concern poor governance or military conflict (e.g. state collapse, interstate conflict and large-scale involuntary migration). No doubt this reflects the ongoing conflicts in the Middle East and various parts of Africa, and the destabilising political impacts of the mass migration of displaced people. Interestingly, the threat posed by weapons of mass destruction has gradually risen up the risk rankings, at least in terms of potential impact. By contrast, whereas the risks caused by poor economic management and severe income inequality figured very prominently in risk assessments during the immediate aftermath of the global financial crisis, they were largely absent from the top-ranked concerns during 2014–16. The substantial changes in the top-ranked risks over a relatively limited time horizon highlight not only how quickly risk perceptions can adjust but also the wisdom of regular monitoring and re-evaluation.

Along with the grim list of global risks highlighted by the World Economic Forum, New Zealand faces a distinctive set of local risks.[4] In particular, it is exposed to a range of major natural hazards, such as earthquakes, volcanic eruptions, tsunamis and extreme weather events. To be sure, the likelihood of such events varies, as does the scale and scope of their impact. Fortunately, most

Table 2.2 The five top global risks in terms of likelihood and impact, 2014–16

Ranking	2014		2015		2016	
	Likelihood	Impact	Likelihood	Impact	Likelihood	Impact
1st	Interstate conflict with regional consequences	Water crises	Large-scale involuntary migration	Failure of climate-change mitigation and adaptation	Extreme weather events	Weapons of mass destruction
2nd	Extreme weather events	Rapid and massive spread of infectious diseases	Extreme weather events	Weapons of mass destruction	Large-scale involuntary migration	Extreme weather events
3rd	Failure of national governance	Weapons of mass destruction	Failure of climate-change mitigation and adaptation	Water crises	Major natural disaster	Water crises
4th	State collapse or crisis	Interstate conflict with regional consequences	Interstate conflict with regional consequences	Large-scale involuntary migration	Large-scale terrorist attack	Large-scale involuntary migration
5th	High unemployment and underemployment	Failure of climate change mitigation and adaptation	Major natural catastrophes	Severe energy price shocks	Massive incident of data fraud/theft	Failure of climate-change mitigation and adaptation

Source: World Economic Forum, *The Global Risks Report 2017*, 12th edition, Geneva, World Economic Forum, 2017, based on global risk perception surveys conducted in the years indicated.

of the hazards which cause the greatest damage, such as very large eruptions, are infrequent.

Nevertheless, the massive 7.8 earthquake which struck near Kaikoura in the early hours of 14 November 2016 is a stark reminder of this country's vulnerability to destructive seismic events. But so, too, were the Canterbury earthquakes during 2010–11. The latter caused large-scale damage to Christchurch and surrounding communities, with the total cost of the rebuild estimated at $40 billion in 2015 dollars.[5]

To compound matters, New Zealand's economy relies heavily on primary production and is thus vulnerable to adverse impacts from pests and diseases – including those exacerbated by climate change. The economic cost of an outbreak of the highly contagious foot and mouth disease would be immense, with the export of meat and dairy products likely to be severely disrupted for many months, if not a year.

In New Zealand, natural hazards like earthquakes understandably attract much public attention. While their timing cannot be accurately predicted, the likelihood of their occurrence can be estimated. On this basis the scope and scale of the likely damage, including the loss of life in specific places and situations, can be statistically modelled, along with the wider economic and social implications. Significantly, most natural hazards – such as the Canterbury and Kaikoura earthquakes or the Manawatu floods (2004) – produce dramatic and highly visible impacts. The public can readily see, feel or imagine their effects. For such reasons, there are strong political pressures for governments to take such risks seriously. Accordingly, governments typically invest in natural hazards research, take measures to mitigate their effects (e.g. via building codes and planning requirements), and prepare comprehensive emergency responses.[6]

GOVERNMENT FAILURE

Just as policy-makers confront various exogenous risks, so too do they face some notable endogenous risks. Of the threats from within, perhaps the most serious is 'government failure'.[7] Such failures can take many forms: choosing the wrong policy instrument to tackle a problem; choosing a sensible instrument but applying it badly; and choosing to do little or nothing despite good reasons for taking preemptive or remedial action. In all such cases, the policy outcomes will be unsatisfactory. Resources will be used inefficiently, inequitably or unsustainably. Worse, serious failures may result in substantial losses, including deaths and much destruction. As policy failures accumulate, so too will the risk of electoral failure – at least in a representative democracy.

Government failure may occur for many different reasons: poor leadership, internal divisions, ministerial incompetence, insufficient information, poorly funded research and evaluation, inadequate advice, weak oversight, poor systems and processes, undue secrecy, bureaucratic bungling, deficient resources or corrupt practices. Obviously, in some cases failures may have multiple causes.

But there is another aspect or dimension of government failure which warrants attention: this is the failure of an intertemporal nature – namely, a tendency to overlook or give inadequate weight to long-term interests. There are at least two types of policy problems where long-term interests are particularly vulnerable to a presentist bias: those known as 'creeping' problems and those which confront policy-makers with politically unattractive intertemporal trade-offs. These two problem types are often connected. Many creeping problems require intertemporal transfers to ameliorate. That is to say, they entail a non-simultaneous exchange: long-term gain may depend on short-term pain. Hence, while such problems may be solvable in technical terms, they can be hard politically: what is desirable in policy terms lacks electoral appeal. They thus require 'tough calls'. Let us explore more fully the nature of creeping problems and those which generate significant intertemporal trade-offs.

CREEPING PROBLEMS

Creeping problems are also known variously as 'looming', 'slow', 'slow-burner', slow-motion', 'slow-moving' or 'emerging'.[8] As the name suggests, creeping problems tend to emerge gradually and sometimes imperceptibly. They evolve bit by bit and often lack critical thresholds or abrupt tipping points, at least during the early stages of their development. While things deteriorate each year, because the changes are slow and incremental they attract little notice. As a result, they are accepted even though the outcomes are objectionable. Such phenomena are sometimes called 'creeping normality'.

Typically, too, creeping problems display a long time lag between cause and effect. Hence, potentially negative impacts may be on the radar and the risk of significant long-term harm may be evident (at least to the relevant experts). However, such problems generally lack vivid, dramatic or unmistakeable early warning signals which can serve to mobilise public concern, thereby prompting a governmental response; they are often not immediately visible, at least in their early stages, and thus are not fully experienced.

Unfortunately, many creeping problems also exhibit a high degree of path dependence and/or produce cumulative – and non-linear – impacts. They thus become harder and more costly to alleviate with the passage of time. Accordingly, delays in responding may reduce or even eliminate the possibility of low-cost solutions. This means that the burden of managing and mitigating the problem will be shifted onto future citizens and taxpayers. Worse, the failure to intervene early may lead to serious and irreversible damage (e.g. to critical ecosystem services or a nation's social fabric), with huge implications for the wellbeing of future generations. Any attempt to improve anticipatory governance, therefore, must give proper attention to creeping problems and identify ways to ensure that they are not ignored by policy-makers.

Amongst the many contemporary creeping problems facing governments, both in New Zealand and elsewhere, are the following:

- long-term demographic changes, such as population ageing, and their economic, social and political implications;
- increased levels of inequality of income and wealth, and their economic, social and political implications;
- the growing number of refugees and internally displaced persons;
- the spreading obesity pandemic;
- the increasing incidence of antimicrobial resistance;
- the increasing surveillance of individuals

and groups within society arising from the growing collection, recording, storage and analysis of information;

- the gradual commodification of body parts;
- the increase in traffic congestion in major urban areas;
- the rising concentrations of greenhouse gases in the atmosphere and the related acidification of the world's oceans;
- the growing vulnerability of critical infra-structure and other physical assets due to their location in coastal zones which are increasingly at risk because of sea level rise;
- the gradual increase in the frequency of intense precipitation events and related flooding;
- the slow accumulation of toxic chemicals in the environment and hence the food chain;
- the decline in the populations of important pollinators, such as honey bees (e.g. because of the spread of colony collapse disorder);
- the steady increase of microplastics (i.e. tiny plastic particles) in the environment as a result of the breakdown of larger plastic debris or the manufacture and use of microplastics in clothing, cosmetics and industrial processes;
- the gradual loss of freshwater supplies due to the depletion of aquifers, deteriorating water quality, the over-allocation of freshwater

resources, and changing climatic conditions;

- the steady decline in valuable agricultural land due to urbanisation and soil degradation;
- the increasing damage to ecosystem services[9] from pollution, invasive species, soil erosion and the loss of habitats;
- the gradual loss of biodiversity and wilderness areas;
- declining levels of societal and political trust; and
- the growing threat to evidence-informed policy-making from fact-averse political movements, scepticism of experts, post-truth narratives and fake news outlets.

As will be evident from this list, a substantial proportion of creeping problems involve environmental degradation and/or risks to public health. They also cover a number of different types of problem. For instance, some are relatively linear in their progression and impacts while others are non-linear; some are stand-alone while others are strongly interdependent; and while many pose challenges across multiple jurisdictions, some are more localised, affecting certain countries or regions much more than others. For instance, in addition to the items listed above, some of the creeping problems that are particularly relevant to New Zealand include:

- declining rates of home ownership, with long-term implications, for instance, for wealth inequality and elder poverty;
- the gradual spread of microscopic pests, such as various types of algae in streams, rivers and lakes – for instance, didymo (or 'rock snot') and lake snow (or 'lake snot');
- increasing numbers of international tourists (exceeding three million in 2015), with escalating environmental pressures, especially in popular but ecologically vulnerable destinations; and
- the cultural implications of the gradual fall in the proportion of the population who can hold a conversation in te reo Māori.

There are many reasons why governments often fail to address creeping problems expeditiously or effectively.[10] First, the problem may not be detected sufficiently early by the relevant authorities. Alternatively, the nature of the risks may be poorly communicated to those within the policy community who are responsible for taking action. Failures of this nature may be attributed to poor monitoring and insufficient early warning systems, inadequate reporting, ambiguous or conflicting evidence, a lack of imagination (e.g. a failure to think through the possible consequences carefully and logically), a disregard for unexpected or puzzling policy-relevant trends, excessive governmental secrecy, and a human tendency to downplay low-probability, but high-impact, events and underestimate future risks, especially those which may appear to be abstract and speculative or never previously experienced.[11]

Second, there may be attentional deficits within the governmental system and the wider polity (i.e. the phenomenon of 'out of sight, out of mind'). Policy-makers are faced with numerous urgent problems and multiple demands. These can easily distract them and result in only limited attention being given to creeping problems and other longer-term challenges. Princeton psychologist Elke Weber, for instance, highlights how our 'finite pool of worry' can crowd out new or temporally distant concerns, focusing our attention on the issues of immediate concern.[12] Similarly, in the absence of vivid and unambiguous warning signals, there will be little pressure from the public for governments to take precautionary measures or early remedial action. There are ways of improving information flows and policy framing such that the political visibility – if not the urgency – of creeping problems can be raised.[13] But even where this is possible (e.g. via simulations of the concrete future consequences of particular trends or events), it is doubtful whether many creeping problems will ever acquire a high level of public concern, especially during their early stages.

Third, some creeping problems may attract only modest public attention not because they are 'out of sight' but because people find it hard to conceptualise and comprehend that there is a genuine threat of serious harm. In the case of climate change, for instance, small changes in global mean temperatures may appear to be inconsequential. Similarly, carbon dioxide is an odourless and colourless gas which is essential for life on Earth. Many people struggle to understand or accept how relatively modest increases in the atmospheric concentrations of a naturally occurring gas could contribute to massive climate change across the planet.

Fourth, many creeping problems are inter-sectoral or trans-boundary in nature and thus require coordinated responses from several tiers of government and/or from multiple organisations. But securing the necessary coordination is often complicated because of the siloed structure of government departments and agencies and the absence of structures and incentives to deal with systemic and cross-cutting risks. Some creeping problems also cross national borders. Hence, solutions depend on international cooperation. This is often hard to achieve. Climate change is perhaps the best example. It constitutes a global collective action problem. To minimise free-riding by individual nations and to reduce carbon leakage, effective mitigation requires coordinated international measures.

Related to this, many creeping problems are 'wicked' in the sense that they have multiple causes and lack complete or definitive solutions.[14] Additionally, the available strategies to ameliorate them often generate significant intersectoral and intertemporal trade-offs. This brings us to the second, albeit related, type of policy problem where there is a heightened risk that long-term interests will be undervalued and poorly protected.

POLICY PROBLEMS THAT REQUIRE INTERTEMPORAL EXCHANGES

Most policy problems – whether economic, social or environmental – have an intertemporal dimension. Often their effects are felt over many years. Equally, solving problems may require dedicated and prolonged efforts. In some cases, too, the main burdens and benefits may fall in different time periods.

Of course, policy problems – like water contamination, ethnic conflicts, substance abuse, species extinction, asset price bubbles, financial crises, homelessness, an ageing population or increasing rates of obesity – differ markedly in the timing and duration of their effects. Some problems are relatively short-lived. Others are recurrent, sporadic or episodic. Yet others – such as crime, domestic violence, chronic illnesses and family dysfunction – are enduring. Some have persistent or irreversible impacts; others do not.

Policy solutions also differ in their temporal dimensions. Some problems can be solved quickly and effectively, while others require ongoing attempts to ameliorate – perhaps over many generations. Whereas some policies generate a relatively steady and even flow of their respective costs and benefits, others exhibit marked unevenness. Indeed, sometimes there is a pronounced disjunction between the timing of their costs and benefits (or co-benefits) – for instance, with current generations bearing most of the costs while future generations receive a disproportionate share of the benefits. In such circumstances, a non-simultaneous exchange is required. Such exchanges are mostly unidirectional: the costs are disproportionately front-loaded while the benefits are disproportionately back-loaded. In some cases the gap between the flow of costs and benefits may be only a few years. But in other cases – like policies to mitigate climate change, reduce the loss of species or clean up badly polluted rivers and lakes – the lags may be very long, perhaps decades or even centuries. Hence, many of those who bear the burden of such interventions enjoy few of the benefits (or co-benefits). The transfers in such cases are not merely intertemporal, they are also intergenerational.

The costs of policy interventions can take several forms. Often they are fiscal in nature (i.e. higher public expenditure and thus higher taxes). Alternatively, they may be regulatory. For instance, additional burdens may be imposed on specific industries, sectors or consumers in order to change behaviour and reduce certain kinds of economic, social or environmental harm.

There is nothing unusual about non-simultaneous exchanges involving near-term costs and back-loaded benefits. To some degree, all investments, whether public or private, take this form: future returns depend on upfront outlays. But whenever significant public investments are required, there is a risk that governments will underinvest – and almost certainly a greater risk of underinvestment than overinvestment. That is to say, because of the disjunction between the respective flows of costs and benefits they may be unwilling for electoral reasons to take the necessary gamble. Other things being equal, the longer the delay between the imposition of the costs and the realisation of the benefits, the more reluctant governments will be to make the required investment.

Of course, investments differ greatly in their characteristics. While the *timing* of their intertemporal payoffs can pose political challenges, there are other features which can contribute to – and exacerbate – such difficulties. These characteristics include: a) the intragenerational and sectoral impacts of the investment; b) the visibility of the impacts; c) the commensurability of the 'goods' at stake (i.e., whether they can be reliably compared using a common unit of measurement, such as money); and d) the degree of certainty about the policy outcomes. With this in mind, investment-type solutions are especially problematic politically when one or more of the following conditions apply:

1. there is a significant gap between the timing of the costs and benefits (or co-benefits) of the investment;
2. the costs fall disproportionately on powerful organised groups while the benefits are spread more evenly across the population; and/or the costs fall largely on groups which enjoy few of the benefits; and/or there is greater clarity about the losers than the winners;
3. the risks or effects of the policy problem are not readily observable, specific, concrete or self-evident while the costs of the investment are much more transparent, direct and obvious;
4. the costs and benefits of the investment are largely incommensurable – in particular,

the costs are mainly financial or material in nature while the benefits are predominantly non-financial and more intangible (e.g. protecting little known species, unique ecosystems, historical sites or other cultural treasures); and

5. there is much more certainty about the nature, timing and magnitude of the costs than about the benefits.

There are at least two main reasons why the benefits of an investment-type policy might be less certain than the costs.

Causal uncertainty

The first relates to causal mechanisms – that is, the relationships between policy inputs, outputs and outcomes. Normally, our knowledge of how and where the costs will fall is much better than our understanding of the causal mechanisms through which the policy is supposed to deliver its benefits. Equally, our understanding of causation varies across different policy domains and types of investment.

Broadly speaking, investments in the field of social policy entail greater causal uncertainty than those involving physical assets.[15] For instance, in most areas of social policy (e.g. education, health care and family services) the chains of policy causation from a specific intervention to actual outcomes are multiple, complex, and only modestly understood.[16] Also, many of the variables that affect the policy's performance – including the various behavioural responses to the intervention – cannot be fully controlled. It is thus difficult to be sure exactly what the long-term social outcomes will be. For such reasons, the actual results, to the extent these can be subsequently identified (e.g. a reduced crime rate, greater social mobility, less poverty or improved health status), may differ markedly from those expected.

But even in the case of investments in physical assets such as long-term infrastructure (e.g. roads, airports, water services and irrigation schemes), significant uncertainties may arise. For instance, the project may involve new materials or untested technologies or may generate significant engineering challenges because of the nature of the terrain. Alternatively, technological changes may render the new infrastructure much less cost-effective than forecast or alter usage in unexpected ways. Other things being equal, the uncertainty over outcomes will increase as the causal complexity and uncertainty intensifies. And, other things being equal, such complexity and uncertainty will rise as time horizons lengthen.

Political sustainability

The level of certainty is not only influenced by the complexity of the causal pathways or the related technical feasibility of the proposed solution. Another problem may arise from doubts over the political sustainability, and hence the durability, of the intervention. In this regard, many investments – and especially those with long timeframes – encounter the challenge of dynamic or time inconsistency or what is sometimes called the compliance, assurance or commitment problem.[17] To be effective, investments must often be sustained over lengthy periods, including multiple electoral cycles. Yet democratic governments cannot readily bind their successors. Their investments are thus at the mercy of future policy-makers, some of whom may doubt the merits of their predecessors' decisions. A crucial problem, therefore, is how to secure a durable political bargain – whether *explicit* (as, for example, with respect to the policy arrangements since 1993 for New Zealand superannuation) or *implicit* (such as the long-standing cross-party support in New Zealand for the state to be the dominant funder of health care).[18]

As a general rule, the risk of dynamic inconsistency will be greater when an investment is controversial and/or is readily reversible (e.g. because the resources in question are fungible and transferable, and there are few sunk costs).[19] Plainly, investments differ on both counts. The level of political controversy is likely to vary according to their distributional impacts, evidential basis, causal complexity, and the nature of the ethical values at stake, including the commensurability or otherwise of the 'goods' in question. The degree of reversibility will depend on the attributes of the investment.

Overall, investments in major infrastructure assets, such as power stations, sewage treatment plants or roading networks, are much less reversible than those which take the form of new environmental taxes, extra levies to pre-fund the cost of future retirement incomes or new health and safety standards. To be sure, the construction and utilisation of new infrastructure assets can be halted, temporarily or permanently. But once such assets are completed and fully operational, there will inevitably be strong pressures to use them and maintain them, even if their original construction was fiercely contested. By contrast, where investments are technically reversible, their durability will be more problematic – all the more so if the electoral costs of reversal are low.

Understandably, governments are likely to consider the political sustainability and reversibility of an investment in their deliberations about whether to proceed. Where the risks of future policy reversals are high, policy-makers will naturally be more reluctant to embark on a new investment. Yet if they choose to do nothing or take only half-hearted measures, significant societal benefits could be foregone or greater damage inflicted.

Take the case of climate change. In both Australia and New Zealand there were lengthy debates during the 1990s and early 2000s over the introduction of price-based policies to reduce greenhouse gas emissions. On both sides of the Tasman, successive governments repeatedly delayed taking action. They also made decisions only to reverse them again shortly afterwards in the face of strong political opposition. Eventually, an emissions trading scheme was introduced in New Zealand while a carbon tax was subsequently implemented in Australia. In both cases, the initial schemes were modest and transitional. The near-term costs were limited. Yet in both cases the major opposition parties found reasons to object, and when given the opportunity of governmental office, they either watered down the original proposals (as happened in New Zealand) or terminated the measures altogether (as occurred in Australia).[20]

Implications
Experiences of this nature raise a number of questions regarding the quest for better anticipatory

governance. One of these is how governments can build multi-party support for long-term investments to tackle major policy problems, thereby enhancing their likely effectiveness and durability. How, in other words, can policy-makers negotiate durable bargains?[21] No doubt, part of the answer lies in the capacity of political leaders to frame policy problems and proposed solutions in ways that can attract broad public support – perhaps because they appeal to long-standing cultural narratives and deeply held values.

Another question is whether there are ways of designing investments so as to make them more costly politically, and/or more difficult technically, to reverse once they have been commenced.[22] In some cases it may be possible to structure policies to enhance public support for their retention. In this way the political costs of subsequent policy reversals will be increased, thereby reducing their likelihood.

To illustrate with respect to social assistance arrangements: when the benefits provided by governments to individuals who are sick, injured, unemployed or retired are linked (at least partially) to their previous contributions (e.g. via a social insurance scheme like accident compensation), they will naturally feel of sense of entitlement to the benefits they obtain from the state. Accordingly, any move by a future government to alter the policy framework – whether in terms of eligibility criteria or levels of assistance – is likely to face stiff political resistance. Against this, where social assistance is tax-funded and there is no linkage between contributions and payments, the sense of entitlement is diminished. Public opposition to reform, therefore, will tend to be lower.

Many investments, however, cannot easily be structured in ways that improve their long-term political support, credibility or durability. Some investments are bound to be controversial because they involve a fundamental clash of politically salient values or interests. Others may be difficult to sustain because the assets generated are fungible, and thus are technically easy to dismantle, transfer or re-allocate. Nevertheless, it will often be possible to incorporate commitment devices into policies, thereby making them more difficult or costly to alter or abandon. Various types of commitment devices will be considered in Chapter 5.

OTHER CAUSES OF THE PRESENTIST BIAS

Thus far this chapter has discussed some of the reasons why a presentist bias occurs in policy-making and why particular kinds of policy problems might be more prone to such a bias. Attention has been given to the role played by policy complexity, uncertainty (e.g. regarding the causal pathways between policy inputs, outputs and outcomes), the temporal asymmetry of costs and benefits, the nature of the informational environment, the incommensurability of the 'goods' at stake, the difficulties of securing durable political bargains – and hence the potential for a compliance problem and dynamic inconsistency. Such considerations point to the presentist bias being a complex phenomenon with multiple causes. Yet only some of the causes have been touched upon so far. While a proper treatment of this topic is not possible here, several other factors which contribute to short-termist policy-making deserve brief mention: the human condition, politically salient asymmetries, ideological polarisation, and low levels of societal trust.

The human condition

Most economic theory assumes that people discount the future – at least to some extent.[23] In other words, people tend to be impatient: they prefer things sooner rather than later. For such reasons, the *timing* of a policy's respective costs and benefits can be expected to affect its electoral appeal. Having said this, there are many reasons why people discount the future. One of these is having a positive pure time preference (i.e. valuing things in the future less than having the same things today). But the evidence suggests that time-preference discount rates are generally low.[24] Often, other factors have a greater effect on individuals' discount rates. These include the level of uncertainty and risk, the nature of the opportunity costs at stake, and the fact that distant outcomes may not receive much attention (i.e. they are undervalued because they are distant or overlooked, not because they are thought to lack worth). There is also evidence that individuals' financial circumstances may influence their time horizons and intertemporal preferences: poverty, for instance, can impede cognitive function and encourage short-termist thinking and behaviour.[25]

Related to this is the matter of how individuals look ahead and think about themselves in future time periods – for instance, Time 1, Time 2, Time 3 and so on – and how such perceptions affect their intertemporal decision-making.[26] The evidence suggests that people regard their 'future selves' as distant or even outside of themselves, almost as if they belong to a different person. In effect, they treat their future selves as strangers. To the extent that people value strangers less than they value themselves, there is an obvious implication: they will place less value on their future selves than their current selves.[27] Of course, people are not completely indifferent to their future wellbeing or that of their children and society. Nor are they generally unconcerned about 'lifetime transcending interests', such as justice and sustainability. But there is clearly a risk that people will downgrade or devalue things that are perceived to be temporally distant, strange or unfamiliar. Equally, there is a risk of selective moral disengagement, with individuals questioning the likelihood of, and minimising their personal responsibility for, future harms.[28]

Recent findings in the fields of cognitive psychology, social psychology and behavioural economics are highly pertinent in this regard. There is good evidence, for instance, that human behaviour is affected by a raft of deep-seated psychological processes, cognitive biases and heuristics (i.e. mental short-cuts, rules of thumb and educated guesses).[29] In other words, various ingrained habits and deeply rooted traits, whether learned or hard-wired via evolutionary processes, influence how people reason and behave, including how they think about, anticipate and value the future. On the whole, when individuals are confronted with intertemporal choices, these psychological processes and biases tilt their preferences and behaviours towards the present. Such findings are relevant not merely for decision-making by individuals acting independently but also for collective processes, such as democratic governance. Having said this, the deliberative mechanisms and public debate that are fundamental to democratic institutions can help to counter the negative impacts of various cognitive biases, not least by exposing all assumptions, proposals and propositions to rigorous scrutiny. Of course, this also means that the quality of such scrutiny matters.

Politically salient asymmetries
There are a variety of asymmetries which are politically salient and which affect intertemporal policy-making. In each case they tend to reinforce a presentist bias. One of these asymmetries, as discussed previously, is the temporal disjunction between the flow of costs and benefits. Another is the voting asymmetry: current generations have voting rights, future generations do not. Yet the decisions of current generations can profoundly affect the wellbeing of future generations. Despite this, future generations have no means by which to hold current generations to account. In the words of the report of the World Commission on Environment and Development in 1987: 'We act as we do because we can get away with it: future generations do not vote; they have no political or financial power; they cannot challenge our decisions.'[30] An important question, then, is whether there are ways to increase the extent to which governments can be held accountable for their long-term thinking – or lack thereof.

Yet another politically salient asymmetry arises from the structure of competing interests. In some policy contexts, there are strong pressures for short-termist decisions, not primarily because effective solutions depend on non-simultaneous exchanges, but because well-organised and concentrated interests are pitted against poorly organised and diffuse interests. For instance, powerful companies or industries may be opposed by weak consumer lobbies. Typically, the voices and votes representing long-term interests are less influential and less well resourced than those representing short-term interests.

Finally, various accounting asymmetries affect intertemporal decision-making, albeit often unconsciously. Under current accounting rules, only some types of costs and benefits are recorded and reported. Whereas firms are required to report annually on their financial performance, they are not obliged to report on the social and environmental impacts of their activities.[31] Likewise, at the governmental level: whereas manufactured (or built) capital and financial capital is regularly valued and accounted for, other types of capital – notably, natural, human and social capital – are not. Accounting asymmetries of this nature matter.[32] They affect how policy-makers and citizens perceive the world, assess progress, and judge governmental performance. Costs and benefits that are measured count; those that are not measured generally don't.

Of course, there are good reasons why some costs and benefits are not comprehensively or regularly measured, reported and valued: doing so poses formidable conceptual and methodological challenges. The measurement and valuing of ecosystem services provides one such example. But the absence of integrated and holistic accounting has consequences. It means that some things – like environmental interests – tend to be devalued. Disproportionately, such things are future-oriented.

Ideological polarisation
Protecting long-term interests requires prudent and durable political bargains. Negotiating such bargains is easier when a nation's political elites are in broad agreement, both about their desired goals and the means to achieve such goals. Commonly held values and shared mental models about the way policies influence outcomes facilitate cross-party agreements on major policy issues, including those where intertemporal trade-offs are to the fore. Equally, securing political agreement at the elite level is more likely when there is a broad societal consensus on policy goals and priorities. By contrast, if societal divisions are deep and entrenched, political parties are strongly polarised

and/or there are powerful populist currents, striking cross-party deals is much harder – as highlighted in recent years in the United States.[33] Amongst other things, ideological polarisation undermines political trust, increases opportunistic behaviour and enhances the risks of dynamic inconsistency. In so doing, it exacerbates the difficulties of tackling long-term policy challenges and reinforces the propensity for short-termist decisions.

Low political trust

Low-trust environments are bad for protecting future interests. When citizens distrust their politicians they are more reluctant to support policies that involve non-simultaneous exchanges. By contrast, where trust is high they will more readily accept the logic of intertemporal bargains and are less likely to penalise governments that implement such strategies.[34] In effect, political trust increases the safe electoral space within which governments make their decisions. It thus represents an important intangible asset. In the language of transaction cost analysis, it constitutes a 'specific asset'.[35] As such, trust plays a vital role within the political system. It provides the glue that enables long-term deals to be struck. It also increases the chances that they will stick. In so doing, it helps mitigate the presentist bias.

Significantly, there is evidence that levels of trust in a society are related to the distribution of income and wealth: the more unequal a society, the lower the level of trust.[36] Understandably, levels of political trust are also influenced by governmental performance and the degree of corruption.[37] Governments that are inefficient and corrupt are not trusted. Such considerations are highly relevant to the quest for sound anticipatory governance. They point to the need to tackle gross inequalities, foster shared goals and values, improve governmental effectiveness and take active measures to minimise corrupt practices.

CONCLUSION

Given the preceding analysis, what kinds of long-term interests are most likely to be at risk?[38] Put differently, where and when can governments be expected to underinvest in protecting future interests?

Leaving aside the wider policy-making context (e.g. the degree of ideological polarisation and the level of political trust), governments are most likely to short-change the future when the following conditions apply:

1. there is a potentially serious problem on the horizon but the informational environment is not conducive to building public support for effective policy responses (e.g. because

of the lack of early warning signals or other information that voters can readily grasp and which demands their attention);

2. solving the problem requires a non-simultaneous exchange involving 'pain today for gain tomorrow';

3. there is expected to be a long lag between the 'pain' and the 'gain';

4. there is uncertainty over the likely effectiveness of the proposed solution (e.g. because causal pathways are complex or poorly understood);

5. powerful interests are opposed to the most effective solution (e.g. because they will bear a disproportionate share of the near-term costs);

6. there is doubt over the political sustainability of the proposed investment (e.g. because it is controversial and/or readily reversible);

7. some of the 'goods' at stake are incommensurable; and

8. delays in responding to a problem will increase the costs of addressing it in the future and/or result in serious and irreversible harm.

The policy implications of such a list should be clear: amongst the long-term interests most at risk in a democratic context (and probably also non-democratic ones) are those of an environmental and social nature. Such interests, of course, also have significant economic dimensions: rectifying environmental damage imposes costs; and poor social outcomes have negative fiscal impacts.

For many reasons, long-term *environmental* interests are particularly vulnerable to short-termist decision-making.[39] Frequently, the degradation and destruction of environmental 'goods', such as ecosystem services, is slow and imperceptible. Often, too, the warning signals of future dangers and losses are masked. Hence, some environmental problems remain largely out of sight and out of mind for many years. Additionally, the relevant causal pathways, path dependencies, cumulative effects and tipping points may be poorly understood. Precisely what is at stake, therefore, may not be clear – until it is too late.

Further, many of the expected harms – whether in the form of a loss of species or unique landscapes – are intangible. They may also be spatially and temporally distant – and perhaps culturally unfamiliar. For various reasons, both the intrinsic and instrumental value of environmental 'goods' can be hard to ascertain. Sometimes, non-monetary or non-economic values are difficult for people to grasp. Equally, calculating the monetary value of particular environmental interests (e.g. specific ecosystem services) is complex. And such calculations depend heavily on the methodologies employed and the discount rate applied. By contrast, it is generally much easier to calculate the costs of intervening to protect the environmental values (whether intrinsic or instrumental) which are at risk. To compound matters, such costs are relatively immediate, visible and direct. And those who will bear them are often easy to identify – and they generally know who they are or they quickly find out.

For all these reasons, the task of protecting long-term environmental interests is particularly demanding. It is here that the risks of a presentist bias in democratic decision-making are often the greatest. It is here, therefore, where those seeking to safeguard the future through better anticipatory governance must devote special attention.

3. THE ATTRIBUTES OF ANTICIPATORY GOVERNANCE

The politician ... looks to the next election, the statesman to the next generation, and philosophy to the indefinite future.

— John Rawls[1]

We must get ahead of events or we risk being overtaken by them.

— Leon Fuerth and Evan Faber[2]

The preceding chapters have highlighted the risk of policy-makers giving undue weight to short-term considerations and the need to enhance anticipatory governance. But what are the attributes or hallmarks of such governance and how can it be encouraged?

Anticipatory governance is an evolving concept. At present, it lacks a widely agreed definition or set of criteria.[3] While its roots lie in horizon-scanning, scenario-planning and adaptive management, the concept is increasingly being employed in other fields and its scope and meaning have broadened. Unsurprisingly, therefore, scholars around the world have applied it in somewhat different ways.

Leon Fuerth and Evan Faber argue that anticipatory governance is 'a systems-based approach for enabling governance to cope with accelerating, complex forms of change'.[4] They stress the importance of systems thinking, a reliance on foresight methods, the close coupling of foresight and day-to-day policy-making, a preference for network-based modes of problem-solving, and the vital role of monitoring and feedback. Anticipatory governance, they contend, is marked by a focus on emerging issues and the registering and tracking of events that are 'just barely visible at the event horizon'.[5] It recognises the value of self-organising and a reliance on emergent properties and processes to 'deal with the unexpected and discontinuous'.[6] And it stresses the importance of incremental adjustment and the 'ongoing evaluation, reassessment, and recalibration of policies in order to prevent breakdowns and systems failures' and respond effectively to significant exogenous shocks or the emergence of new technologies.[7]

A narrower and more focused definition is proffered by David Guston.[8] From Guston's perspective, anticipatory governance is about preparing societies for the large-scale, non-linear impacts of major scientific discoveries and disruptive technologies. The emphasis is not so much on predicting the future or what has been called 'predict and plan' (i.e., forecasting what is expected and then developing plans to match the most likely scenario).[9] Rather, anticipatory governance means accepting that some aspects of the future are unknowable and many futures are possible. Hence, governments must prepare for, and be in a position to respond to, whatever eventuates. In Guston's view, this means, amongst other things, designing institutions that are capable of accommodating, innovating and coping well with the impacts of major technological advances. And this requires good foresight, including robust techno-scientific assessment regimes, policy flexibility and adaptive management.

Yet other scholars highlight other features of anticipatory governance.[10] Some, for instance, emphasise the importance of public engagement, participatory mechanisms and bottom-up processes. Others underscore the vital role of precautionary and prudential policy approaches. Alternatively, they stress the normative dimension, such as the need for ethical leadership and responsible political management in the face of deep uncertainty, rapid change and transformative scientific developments. Arguably, all these discrete elements are important. What matters is the total package.

EIGHT CORE ATTRIBUTES

With such considerations in mind, sound anticipatory governance is characterised by at least eight attributes, as depicted in Figure 3.1. It is forward-looking, vigilant, proactive, holistic and systems-oriented, and adaptive – with the objective of being prepared and having thought through plausible future scenarios and outcomes. Additionally, it fosters resilience and sustainability, it favours a participatory approach to decision-making, and it seeks to embed long-term interests and future-focused concerns in day-to-day decision-making. A brief exploration of these attributes follows.

Forward-looking

Anticipatory governance values foresight. It regularly scans the horizon for warning signals, as well as new, but often unexpected, opportunities. It imagines alternative futures and scrutinises their likelihood and desirability. It considers a range of scenarios, including worse-case outcomes. It assesses the long-term consequences of today's decisions and events, seeking to minimise future harms as cost-effectively as possible. It looks out

Fig 3.1 The attributes of anticipatory governance

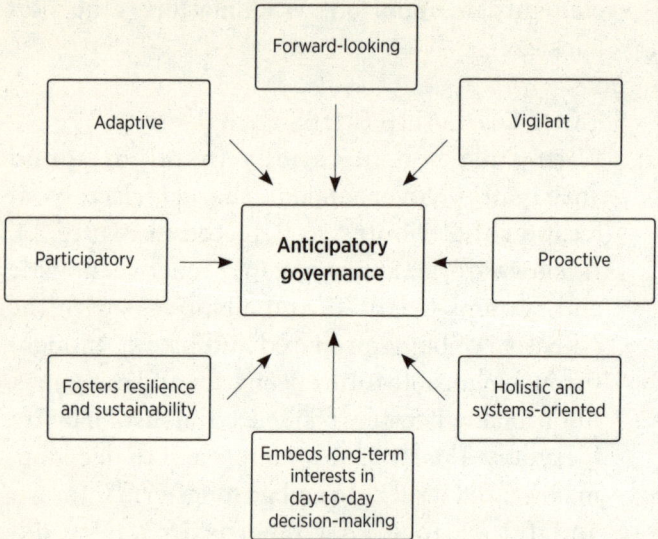

over extended time horizons, not merely years, but rather decades and sometimes centuries, depending on the nature of the issue.

Vigilant
Anticipatory governance is alert to multiple risks, including those of a systemic nature. In the face of uncertainty it takes a precautionary approach. Amongst other things, this means placing the burden of proof on the advocates of a potentially risky action or policy initiative to demonstrate

that the threat of harm is low and justified.[11] In this regard, an anticipatory approach is wary of confident predictions and technological optimism (i.e. the idea that whatever messes we might make we will find the means to fix them). It is ever mindful of emerging issues and creeping problems and their potential to be overlooked, underestimated and ignored. Equally, it takes seriously the dangers posed by policy legacies, path dependence, interdependencies, cumulative effects, tipping points, changing risk profiles, 'black swan' events and what have recently been called 'black elephants'.[12] Hence, it seeks wherever possible to identify future threats and implement effective responses before their negative consequences are realised (e.g. through early warning systems and active listening for signals of failure, emerging hazards, new scientific evidence and technological risks). It conducts regular 'stress tests' to ascertain the robustness of current institutional, policy and regulatory settings. And it develops the capability and tools for rigorous risk management. It is especially alert to the risks of government failure. In particular, it draws on the insights of behavioural economics and social psychology, most notably the influence of cognitive biases on risk assessment and decision-making. In so doing, it recognises the dangers of selective moral disengagement, political myopia, collective amnesia and group think.

Proactive

Anticipatory governance seeks to shape the future, not merely react and respond. It values preparedness and readiness. As a general rule, it favours prevention over cure, and pre-emptive measures over remedial action. Accordingly, it evaluates low-cost measures to help prevent desirable options being inadvertently foreclosed. To this end, it invests heavily in research and evaluation, and seeks high-quality evidence. It makes policy monitoring and regular feedback a priority. It encourages self-evaluation and organisational learning. It pursues continuous improvement. It fosters in-depth public debate on important policy issues. Above all, it celebrates creativity, curiosity and imaginative reflection.

Holistic and systems-oriented

Anticipatory governance endorses a holistic approach to policy analysis and performance assessment. It favours systems-based thinking and methodologies. It acknowledges the existence of manifold policy interdependencies. Hence, it is mindful of the need in many cases for trans-jurisdictional and cross-agency solutions. Similarly, it recognises the value of relying on multiple performance measures and indicators, including those which capture changes in stocks as well as flows. In this regard, it acknowledges the vital importance of many different kinds of capital assets – not merely financial and manufactured capital, but also natural, human, intellectual and social capital. For such reasons, it focuses not only on fiscal deficits, but also on social, ecological and democratic deficits. Equally, it acknowledges the threat posed by deficits in adaptive capacity, all the more so in an era of remarkable technological advances, unprecedented environmental changes and multiple hazards.[13]

Adaptive

In protecting future interests, anticipatory governance seeks robust, yet flexible, democratic institutions and processes. It accepts the fundamental reality of uncertainty and does not yearn for false certainties. Instead, it embraces the need, given a dynamic and unpredictable world, for anticipatory planning, regular incremental change and adaptive management.[14] It remains open to the possibility of, and need for, transformative change to adjust to new realities as the conditions change beyond the capacities of existing institutions and processes. In so doing, it plans for a range of contingencies, it seeks to preserve future options, and it welcomes flexible, no-regrets strategies (i.e. near-term, cost-effective measures that can be readily adapted over time as events unfold).

Anticipatory governance also recognises that while the past profoundly affects the future, evidence based on previous events and patterns may provide little guidance to the future. After all, long-standing trends may cease and gradual adjustments may be superseded by non-linear changes. Disruptive technologies, natural disasters, systemic financial failures, abrupt shifts (e.g. in climatic conditions) and the role played by emergence (with emergent structures, properties and processes) may fundamentally alter a nation's trajectory. Policy-makers, therefore, cannot rely only on existing performance data or projections based on recent trends.[15] At the same time, currently available data are not irrelevant. Indeed, such data are extremely useful for assessing whether particular long-term interests are being adequately protected.

Fosters resilience and sustainability
Anticipatory governance recognises a wide range of vulnerabilities and the critical importance of resilience and sustainability. Both concepts, of course, are broad, complex and controversial. Their relevance spans multiple policy domains and institutional contexts.

Take, for instance, the idea of resilience.[16] This includes notions of flexibility and adaptability, the capacity to bounce back to a desired equilibrium after a shock, and the ability to absorb chronic stresses or abrupt impacts without serious damage or disruption.[17] Resilience has many specific features: robustness, redundancy, resourcefulness, responsiveness, and the capacity to recover or recuperate.[18] As defined in the United Nations International Strategy for Disaster Reduction, it means:

The ability of a system, community or society exposed to hazards to resist, absorb, accommodate to and recover from the effects of a hazard in a timely and efficient manner, including through the preservation and restoration of its essential basic structures and functions.[19]

Sustainability, likewise, is a crucial goal in many policy areas. Yet the concept has multiple and competing definitions, with many contrasting specifications of what ought to be sustained and by what means.[20] Amongst the many distinctions are those between 'strong' and 'weak' sustainability. But even here different approaches abound. Despite this, as Herbert Stein, a leading American economist, famously put it: 'If something cannot go on forever, it will stop.' Likewise, 'trends that can't continue, won't'. Anticipatory governance recognises such realities and adjusts policy settings accordingly – ideally, long before critical thresholds are crossed or policy 'crunches' arrive.

Participatory

Public engagement and participation are critical for sound anticipatory governance for at least three reasons. First, citizens are a huge repository of relevant information and knowledge. As such, they constitute an essential and irreplaceable part of the 'sensory system' of democratic governance – filtering signals, detecting problems, highlighting issues, identifying options and providing feedback. Ultimately, good governance depends on vigorous democratic institutions and active, informed and engaged citizens.

Second, policy-makers need public support in order to implement non-simultaneous exchanges and take proactive measures to protect future interests. Fostering such support requires a strategic approach to enhancing citizens' understanding of major long-term issues and involving them in the formulation and scrutiny of policy options. Participatory modes of decision-making, especially those involving deliberative processes (such as collaborative governance and citizens' juries), enable policy learning and can extend participants' time horizons.[21] They also provide a means for building a greater measure of consensus on acceptable levels of risk. But for such approaches to work well, relevant, high-quality information is vital.

Third, and related to this, when people have a sense of 'ownership' of the decisions made by their governments and believe they have a stake in their society, they are more likely to trust their leaders and have confidence in their system of governance. Participation, in other words, strengthens legitimacy. Moreover, as argued in Chapter 2, higher levels of public trust increase the safe electoral space within which governments operate and facilitate intertemporal bargains.

Embeds long-term interests in day-to-day decision-making

Because it recognises the risk of a presentist bias in policy-making, anticipatory governance chooses institutional mechanisms, analytical tools, policy frameworks and commitment devices which bring the long term into short-term focus and ensure that tomorrow's interests are actively considered – and properly represented – in today's decisions. The goal, in short, is to embed the future in the present, thereby ameliorating the risk of short-sighted or myopic decisions.

Of course, these many attributes of anticipatory governance are ambitious and demanding. They serve as an ideal to which governments should aspire. For understandable reasons, they will often fall short.

ASSESSING THE QUALITY OF ANTICIPATORY GOVERNANCE

With such attributes in mind, how might the quality of anticipatory governance be assessed? What specific criteria or standards should be employed?

To start with, any such assessment is but one part of the wider task of judging the overall quality of governmental institutions and systems of public governance. While good governance must be anticipatory, it must also be many other things: legal, honest, legitimate, democratic, effective, efficient, fair, accountable, and much else.[22]

Moreover, there is no sharp boundary delineating the *anticipatory* component of good governance. Anticipatory governance is not simply about good planning for the future. And even if it were, good planning is demanding and requires many things: comprehensive and reliable information, excellent monitoring and reporting, capable staff, adequate resources, sound analytical tools and robust decision-making processes. Accordingly, assessments of anticipatory governance take us well beyond the confines of specific activities like strategic planning, foresight methods, risk management or emergency management.

Further, all assessments of the quality of governance involve the exercise of judgement. Inevitably, therefore, they are controversial. In the case of anticipatory governance, the challenges are particularly marked.

For one thing, our knowledge base is limited. We lack the luxury of jumping decades or centuries forward in time and then looking back to assess how well the governments of the early twenty-first century prepared for, and navigated, the future. Historians many generations from now will enjoy the benefit of such hindsight, but we do not. Hence, any assessment today will necessarily be imperfect and incomplete.

For another, while numerous criteria for assessing anticipatory governance can be suggested, some are hard to put into operation. Take, for example, the concept of resilience. Assessing the resilience of systems, governments, individual public institutions, societies or communities is far from straightforward. What criteria, for example, should be used to assess the capacity of an economy to absorb a major financial shock or a community to cope with a large seismic event? How much cushion against possible adverse outcomes is desirable? How much in-built redundancy should there be? What level of risk is acceptable? How much is it reasonable to spend on risk reduction? And who should be the judge? While answers to such questions are clearly possible, every approach is likely to be problematic.

Next, we should be wary of seeking a single aggregate indicator or composite measure of the quality of anticipatory governance. There are simply too many different variables and they cover too many different kinds of performance. Instead, a better approach would be to employ a performance dashboard with multiple criteria and a simple scoring regime. While lacking the simplicity of a single metric, this approach nonetheless enables comparisons over time and between governments.

As to the nature of the relevant criteria, there is a need for a mix of substantive and procedural measures. Of particular importance are criteria which capture the extent to which governments employ analytical tools, policy frameworks and decision-making procedures that encourage reflection on long-term policy issues and incentivise the protection of future interests. This, of course, prompts many questions. How, for instance, can the 'voice' of the future be adequately represented in day-to-day decision-making? How can political incentives be altered so that governments are likely to take creeping problems more seriously? How can policy-makers be encouraged to make 'hard calls'? How can we reduce the risk of immediate concerns crowding out or constantly trumping future interests?

There are no simple solutions. But there are ways of structuring institutional arrangements, analytical frameworks and political processes such that long-term considerations are more likely to figure in the decision-making calculus.[23] These include:

- requiring policy-makers to have regard to the best available scientific evidence;
- ensuring a high level of transparency in decision-making at all levels of government;
- using analytical frameworks to formulate policy advice that capture the full range of likely costs and benefits (e.g. direct and indirect, tangible and intangible, etc.);
- ensuring that the impact of choosing different discount rates is fully transparent;
- instituting commitment devices that require the policy 'system' to conduct regular foresight exercises, undertake periodic long-term forecasts and projections, carry out regular stress tests and risk assessments, and develop long-term plans (e.g. for conservation, infrastructure and other forms of public investment);
- requiring governments to set explicit, meaningful and measurable targets (and related milestones) for improving outcomes, especially regarding significant long-term policy challenges, and to report progress on a regular basis;

- establishing independent future-oriented institutions to provide an authoritative 'voice' for otherwise poorly represented long-term interests;
- encouraging respectful deliberation and informed, reasoned debate via the use of moderated participatory mechanisms, multi-stakeholder forums and collaborative policy-making processes;
- nurturing trust, shared values and common goals; and
- seeking cross-party agreements where durable long-term commitments are needed to address major policy problems.

Table 3.1 outlines some suggested criteria for assessing the quality of anticipatory governance. There are seven broad categories: overarching principles; planning processes and foresight; policy and regulatory frameworks; the representation of future-oriented interests; performance measures and reporting; resilience, risk management and emergency management; and mechanisms for negotiating durable political bargains. Within each category one or more specific criteria are suggested. But Table 3.1 is far from exhaustive. Under each of the seven categories more criteria (and examples) could be added – such as those of relevance to different tiers of government, specific institutions or discrete policy domains.

Table 3.1 Criteria for assessing the quality of anticipatory governance

Category of criteria	Specific criteria
Overarching principles	Policy settings should be consistent with well-established principles of intergenerational justice.
	The principle of sustainability should be embedded in all relevant policy frameworks.
	Policy-makers across all levels of government should be obliged to adhere to the precautionary principle.
	Public sector managers should be required to exercise proper stewardship (or kaitiakitanga) of their organisations.
Planning processes and foresight	Governments should be required to undertake long-term planning across the full range of their investment activities.
	There should be robust foresight processes at all levels of government, including requirements for independent bodies to report periodically on major risks and vulnerabilities, as well as emerging issues, across all policy domains.
Policy and regulatory frameworks	Policy options should be assessed using holistic analytical frameworks.
	Targets should be set for major long-term policy goals.
	The long-term costs and benefits of different policy options should be clearly identified and made transparent, based on a range of discount rates.
	Externalities should be properly priced.
	There should be rigorous systems for policy-learning via regular evaluation.
The representation of future-oriented interests	There should be independent public institutions with a legislative mandate to represent specified future-oriented interests.
Performance measures and reporting	There should be comprehensive measures for assessing economic, social and environmental performance across all policy domains.
	There should be comprehensive national balance sheets covering all forms of capital.
Major risks and their management	There should be comprehensive policies for disaster risk reduction and strengthening the resilience of all critical infrastructure and systems.
	There should be future-proofing funds for such things as natural disasters, climate change adaptation and population ageing.
	There should be regular stress tests by public institutions to evaluate their resilience and adaptive capacity.
Mechanisms for negotiating durable political bargains	Participatory and multi-party processes should be employed to develop politically durable solutions for long-term issues.

Source: adapted from J. Boston, 'Anticipatory Governance: How Well is New Zealand Safeguarding the Future?', *Policy Quarterly*, 13, 3 (August 2016), pp.18–20.

The criteria and mechanisms outlined in Table 3.1 are focused primarily on policy frameworks, legislative provisions, institutional arrangements and policy-making processes rather than actual outcomes. In the end, of course, outcomes are critically important. Accordingly, one of the main tests of the quality of anticipatory governance is whether policy-makers are delivering satisfactory outcomes – whether economic, social and environmental – and especially outcomes that are likely to be consistent with the long-term needs and wellbeing of citizens. This is discussed further in Chapter 4.

CONCLUSION

Robust, future-focused policies, institutions and frameworks can be expected to contribute to better results. For one thing, they will ensure that high-quality evidence is produced regularly, thereby enabling citizens and policy-makers to ascertain whether progress is being made towards meeting important long-term societal goals and protecting vital interests. For another, future-focused institutions and processes will encourage and facilitate efforts to improve long-term performance. In short, they will help increase the political demand for better results.

Yet there are no guarantees. Ultimately, sound anticipatory governance depends on capable and alert leaders, vibrant democratic institutions and a vigorous civil society. For these qualities to be realised, citizens must be engaged, discerning, responsible and sometimes courageous. Such a citizenry cannot be manufactured, but it can be nurtured.

4. ASSESSING THE QUALITY OF ANTICIPATORY GOVERNANCE IN NEW ZEALAND

Mō tātou, ā, mō kā uri ā muri ake nei – for us and our children after us
                              – Ngāi Tahu's guiding whakatauāki

How well does New Zealand fare against the suggested criteria outlined in Chapter 3? Is this country well positioned to meet the challenges of the twenty-first century? Do our governance arrangements – including our major political institutions, policy settings and regulatory frameworks – adequately protect long-term interests? What strengths and weaknesses are apparent? What does an assessment through an anticipatory lens reveal, both about our governance structures and our policy outcomes?

To date, there has been no comprehensive or detailed evaluation of the quality of anticipatory governance in New Zealand. There are, however, numerous regular and ad hoc assessments – some official, others unofficial – that cover some of the criteria sketched in Chapter 3. Most of these focus on specific policy domains, such as fiscal policy, health policy, national security, emergency management, public infrastructure and the environment. Nevertheless, they provide a useful indication as to whether important long-term interests are being appropriately safeguarded.

To take a few examples: every three to four years, the Treasury publishes a statement on the country's long-term fiscal position – as is required by Section 26N of the Public Finance Act 1989.[1] Under the Act, such documents must look forward at least forty years. While the Act is silent on their precise contents, the statements are expected to consider, amongst other things, the long-term costs of existing government spending programmes, projected trends in revenue and the fiscal sustainability of current policy settings. Importantly, the analysis and findings are the responsibility of the Secretary to the Treasury, rather than the Minister of Finance, and the Treasury is obliged to employ 'its best professional judgments' in evaluating the fiscal outlook and potential risks.[2] Hence, the resulting documents are independent and authoritative. As such, they provide a useful indication of whether there are significant fiscal challenges on the horizon. Thus far, the Treasury has prepared four statements, the most recent in late 2016.[3]

Also, under Section 26NA of the Public Finance Act, the Treasury is required to produce an investment statement at least every four years. The statement must assess the 'value of the Crown's significant assets and liabilities', indicate how they 'have changed in value over time', and forecast expected changes in their value looking out several years.[4] Again, such statements give policy-makers useful guidance on matters of relevance for the longer term. But currently they cover only a limited range of capital stocks; they do not include, for instance, natural, social or human capital.

Importantly, under Parliament's Standing Orders,[5] both the Treasury's long-term fiscal statements and its investment statements are referred to the Finance and Expenditure Committee for examination. The committee has six months to report on the former statements and two months on the latter, and there are provisions under Standing Orders for the relevant documents to be debated in the House once the committee's reports have been presented. There is thus an opportunity for proper parliamentary scrutiny and accountability.

Many other government departments and agencies produce regular reports which highlight recent trends and developments in their respective policy domains, some of which have major implications for long-term societal outcomes. For instance, the Controller and Auditor-General produces various future-focused reports, such as those on the quality and management of public infrastructure.[6] Likewise, under the Environmental Reporting Act 2015, the Government Statistician and the Secretary for the Environment are required to produce every three years a synthesis report on the state of the country's environment, including biodiversity and ecosystems, the pressures affecting the environment and the impacts of the changing state of the environment on such things as ecological integrity and public health.[7] Additionally, the Act obliges the preparation of regular domain reports covering: the air; the atmosphere and climate; freshwater; land; and the marine environment. As part of the reporting process, there is a requirement to evaluate the state of New Zealand's environment in relation to national and international standards. Assessments of this nature enable judgements to be made about the quality of environmental governance and whether critical long-term environmental interests are at risk.

Aside from official reports, there is a plethora of assessments by university academics, postgraduate students, Crown Research Institutes and non-governmental organisations across a range of policy domains, many of which report on long-term trends and identify looming problems.[8] There are also various in-depth analyses of topics that are highly relevant for evaluations of the quality of anticipatory governance. For instance, a senior Treasury official, Ken Warren, has assessed in recent years the resilience of New Zealand's economy and society, with particular reference to four types of capital – financial, human, social and natural.[9] Likewise, in 2013 Transparency International New Zealand produced a comprehensive report on the accountability and transparency of our democratic institutions, viewed specifically through an integrity lens.[10]

Drawing on studies of this nature and other available data, the remainder of this chapter reviews the quality of anticipatory governance in New Zealand. It begins with observations about the country's governance arrangements (including important policy settings and regulatory frameworks) and then turns to the question of policy outcomes and their long-term implications.

ASSESSING NEW ZEALAND'S GOVERNANCE ARRANGEMENTS USING AN ANTICIPATORY LENS

Based on the criteria outlined in Table 3.1, it is reasonable to conclude that many of New Zealand's governance arrangements are relatively future-focused in the sense that they oblige policy-makers and/or their advisers to assess the long-term implications of current policy settings and to consider the future needs and interests of citizens. In several cases, there are requirements to look ahead at least thirty or forty years. There are, however, some notable gaps. Moreover, it is one thing to embrace future-focused principles, frameworks, procedures and capabilities, and quite another to ensure that they are taken seriously and achieve their intended goals.

The following assessment provides a brief snapshot of the strengths and weaknesses of New Zealand's current governance arrangements, based on the seven broad categories identified in Chapter 3. A fuller treatment must await another occasion.

Overarching principles
Currently, most of the overarching, future-focused principles summarised in Table 3.1 are incorporated into a number of important statutes, particularly those of relevance to fiscal management, resource management and public management. For instance:

- since the Fiscal Responsibility Act 1994, governments have been legally obliged to comply with various principles of fiscal responsibility, including achieving and maintaining prudent levels of public debt;[11]

- under Section 5 of the Resource Management Act 1991, policy-makers are required to 'promote the sustainable management of natural and physical resources'. This includes, under Section 5(2), 'sustaining the potential of natural and physical resources (excluding minerals) to meet the reasonably foreseeable needs of future generations ... safeguarding the life-supporting capacity of air, water, soil, and ecosystems ... and avoiding, remedying, or mitigating any adverse effects of activities on the environment';
- the New Zealand Coastal Policy Statement, mandated under the Resource Management Act, embodies various elements of precaution, including requirements for decision-makers to adopt a long planning horizon (see below);[12] and
- under the State Sector Act 1988, as amended in 2013, the State Services Commissioner is required to promote 'a culture of stewardship in the State services', while departmental chief executives are responsible for 'the stewardship of the department'. Such 'stewardship' is defined as 'the active planning and management of medium- and long-term interests, along with associated advice'. Accordingly, it includes a department's 'medium- and long-term sustainability,

organisational health, capability, and capacity to offer free and frank advice to successive governments'. Significantly, the scope of this 'stewardship' responsibility embraces the assets and liabilities managed by the department, as well as the legislation that it oversees and administers.[13]

Against this, current policy frameworks in New Zealand, even at their best, only enunciate in very broad terms the principles of intergenerational justice that should guide decision-making on issues with major intertemporal implications. There are no requirements, for example, for governments to consider whether their policies are fair from an intergenerational perspective. Nor are governments obliged to assess and report on the intergenerational implications of current policy settings or new policy initiatives, even those which are highly likely to have significant long-term distributional impacts. As might be expected, therefore, no government has sought to develop a composite index of intergenerational fairness or provide periodic evaluations of how their policies are expected to affect the wellbeing of citizens in, say, 30, 50 or 100 years.[14]

Likewise, while a number of statutes oblige policy-makers to take reasonable precautions or to be cautious when evidence is limited or uncertain, such requirements are neither widespread nor exacting. Moreover, there are few explicit references in legislation to a precautionary principle or a precautionary approach.[15] Strikingly, the precautionary principle is not explicitly embraced in the Resource Management Act 1991, although some argue that it is implicit in how the Act is to be implemented (and it is explicitly embraced in the New Zealand Coastal Policy Statement 2010). Importantly, too, there is no requirement for the principle to be applied as part of an integrated risk management framework.[16] Nor are there clear guidelines to help ensure that the principle is implemented in a consistent and rigorous manner across *all* relevant policy domains. This contrasts markedly with the situation in Canada, the European Union and the United States.[17]

Equally, while the principle of sustainability is firmly embraced, especially in the areas of resource management and environmental protection, the application of the principle has generally been at the 'weak' end of the possible spectrum. Thus far, for instance, there has been a general acceptance that manufactured capital can be substituted for natural capital. Similarly, the use of biodiversity offsets in New Zealand is limited and often poorly implemented.[18] Nor have any requirements been enacted to maintain aggregate levels of renewable natural capital or compensate future generations for the loss of non-renewable natural capital (e.g. by increasing stocks of renewable natural capital).[19]

Planning processes and foresight
There are a range of legislative provisions which require policy-makers at various levels of government to consider long-term needs and interests, especially with respect to urban planning and infrastructure investment. For example, under Section 10(1)(b) of the Local Government Act 2002, local authorities are required 'to meet the current *and future* [my emphasis] needs of communities for good-quality local infrastructure, local public services, and performance of regulatory functions'. Under Section 11(A), 'good-quality' is defined as infrastructure, services and performance that are efficient, effective and appropriate to 'present and *anticipated future* [my emphasis] circumstances'. Local authorities are also required to prepare thirty-year infrastructure strategies. Such strategies must identify significant infrastructure issues and how they will be managed. In terms of planning, it has been mandatory since 2002 for local authorities to prepare long-term plans. These plans must cover no less than ten years. With respect to climate change, much longer planning horizons are mandated. For instance, the New Zealand Coastal Policy Statement 2010 obliges local planners to take into

account how the effects of climate change, most notably sea level rise, might affect coastal hazard risk over 'at least a 100-year timeframe'.[20]

Meanwhile, at the central government level, the National Infrastructure Unit (located within the Treasury) is required to prepare periodic plans for the management and planning of public infrastructure over a thirty-year time horizon,[21] as well as documents outlining the government's plans for capital investment over a ten-year time horizon.

Against this, local authorities have been struggling to develop strategies to cope with the expected impacts of climate change, especially the virtual inevitability of substantial sea level rise.[22] The problem here is that risk profiles are not static; they are dynamic and uncertain. They thus require adaptive management, with flexible, evolving strategies.[23] But such approaches are hard politically. Understandably, many citizens, and especially those with vulnerable coastal properties, want certainty. Above all, they want their assets protected – or at least to be fully compensated if such protection is not viable. But this raises fundamental issues about who should bear the risks associated with climate change, what level of risk is acceptable, to what extent various risks can be mitigated (and at what cost), how the residual risk (i.e. the threat that remains once all reasonable efforts have been taken to identify and reduce the risk in question) should be handled, and how the various costs should be shared. Plainly, there are no easy answers.[24] What is clear, however, is that our current institutions and policy frameworks are inadequate. If the test of New Zealand's anticipatory governance arrangements is their capacity to manage effectively the risks and impacts of climate change (and especially sea level rise), there can be little doubt that they will be found wanting.

But there is a related significant weakness: the country's investment in formal foresight processes is limited and compares unfavourably with several other small democracies.[25] Amongst other things, there is no dedicated, high-level foresight unit in central government; there are no requirements for major departments and agencies to conduct regular foresight exercises (e.g. horizon-scanning and scenario-planning), identify creeping problems or formulate strategies to address them; there are no requirements for governments to prepare periodic reports on major long-term issues and how they plan to address them; there is no parliamentary select committee with a specific mandate to tackle future-oriented policy challenges and intergenerational issues; and there is little public investment in assessing the implications – whether economic, social, cultural or environmental – of new technologies.

Policy and regulatory frameworks

In recent years, several major departments – including the Treasury and the departments that make up the 'natural resources sector' (led by the Ministry for the Environment) – have developed more holistic analytical frameworks to guide the formulation of policy advice to governments.[26] The Treasury's Living Standards Framework, for instance, focuses on capital stocks as well as flows, considers a full range of capital stocks, and identifies multiple goals, including sustainability. Employing a framework of this kind is likely to increase the chances of important long-term interests being properly identified and considered in assessing policy options. Other positive features of the current policy-making landscape include: a strong emphasis on policy advice being evidence-based, underscored in recent years by the appointment of chief science advisors in many departments;[27] significant efforts to improve the quality of regulatory frameworks, including regulatory stewardship;[28] the application of rules governing public sector financial management that embody a high level of transparency and ensure that the depreciation of assets is fully costed; and the setting of medium-term targets, via the government's 'Better Public Services' initiative, for improving outcomes in a number of important areas of policy.[29] Also, in July 2016 the government set an ambitious long-term goal in the area of conservation, namely to eradicate all non-native predators within 35 years (i.e. by around 2050) so as to protect the country's indigenous wildlife.

Against this, there are many reasons for concern. To date, the Treasury's Living Standards Framework has had only a modest impact on the advice being tendered by government departments and has yet to receive strong public endorsement from senior ministers. Further, successive governments have been reluctant to develop comprehensive and ambitious strategies to tackle various major long-term policy challenges (e.g. protecting the marine environment, decarbonising the energy and transport systems, and tackling obesity and child poverty). And there has been only slow progress in establishing a system of 'comprehensive wealth' accounting, including national balance sheets which cover a broader range of capital stocks such as natural capital.

The representation of future-oriented interests in the policy process

New Zealand has a number of long-established, legally mandated, independent public officers and institutions which have, as a core part of their role, the representation of future-oriented interests. Amongst these are the Parliamentary

Commissioner for the Environment established in 1986, the Children's Commissioner established in 1989, and the Retirement Commissioner established in 2001. In addition, the Department of Conservation, under Section 6 of the Conservation Act 1987, has explicit responsibilities 'to advocate the conservation of natural and historic resources generally', 'to preserve so far as is practicable all indigenous freshwater fisheries, and protect recreational freshwater fisheries and freshwater fish habitats' and 'to promote the benefits to present and future generations' of, amongst other things, 'the conservation of natural and historic resources generally and the natural and historic resources of New Zealand in particular'.

In recent years, the government has established the Productivity Commission, modelled on its Australian counterpart. While not primarily designed to focus on the long-term, most of the issues which the commission has thus far addressed (e.g. regulatory institutions and practices, the design of social services, urban planning and new models of tertiary education) have major implications for the promotion and protection of future-oriented interests. One concern, however, is whether the commission is giving sufficient weight to the full range of capital assets (including social and natural capital) on which New Zealanders' long-term wellbeing depends.

Aside from this, New Zealand universities have an explicit role, under Section 162(4)(a)(v) of the Education Act, 'as critic and conscience of society', which presumably includes highlighting major societal risks, addressing important intertemporal issues and drawing attention to interests that tend to be poorly represented in political processes, such as those of future generations. Additionally, the Royal Society of New Zealand has a statutory mandate to promote the advancement of science, technology and the humanities. This includes promoting 'public awareness, knowledge, and understanding' of such endeavours and fostering 'a culture that supports' them.[30] Again, such a role must almost certainly include activities that enhance public understanding of long-term risks and vulnerabilities and ways of addressing them.

Of course, it is one thing to have independent 'voices' for the future, it is quite another for such 'voices' to be heard and exercise political influence. Assessing influence is hard, as is evaluating the quality of the advocacy in question. A good case can be made that each of the institutions mentioned above has contributed to a more informed public debate and to policy decisions that better protect long-term interests. Yet the gains often appear to be marginal and the extent to which there is now a more strategic approach to safeguarding New Zealand's future is clearly a matter for debate.[31]

Performance measures and reporting

Comprehensive, relevant and reliable data are critical for protecting current and future interests. Serious gaps in knowledge obviously reduce the capacity of policy-makers to know what is happening, let alone respond in an informed way. Overall, New Zealand has relatively exacting requirements for public agencies to monitor, assess and report performance in their respective areas of responsibility. This includes comprehensive and independent reporting by Statistics New Zealand across multiple policy domains, detailed reporting by the Treasury in relation to fiscal and economic matters, regular scrutiny of public sector performance by the Controller and Auditor-General, and, as noted earlier, a new, more systematic regime of environmental reporting. There are, however, notable gaps. Efforts have been made for several decades to place the Social Report (produced intermittently by the Ministry for Social Development) on a statutory basis. But these have thus far failed. Partly as a result, the 2010 Social Report was not updated until 2016.[32] Further, the monitoring of outcomes in many policy domains is very patchy. This is especially true with respect to many environmental matters, not least because of the limited number of monitoring sites in many parts of the country (e.g. for freshwater and pests).[33]

Major risks and their management

New Zealand has numerous statutes and policies to address major risks, particularly concerning disaster-related risk and emergency management.[34] These deal with natural disasters, such as earthquakes, tsunamis and floods, as well as various man-made hazards, such as threats to biodiversity (e.g. from the introduction of pests and new organisms), technological hazards and threats to national security (e.g. from cyber-attacks, terrorism, regional conflicts, failed states or mass migration). Relevant statutes include the Resource Management Act 1991, the Building Act 2004, the Civil Defence Emergency Management Act 2002, the Local Government Act 2002 and the Earthquake Commission Act 1993. While policy-makers in New Zealand gave only limited attention to the United Nations Hyogo Framework for Action 2005–15, which was designed to strengthen the resilience and capacity of countries and communities to cope with disasters, they have embraced more fully the recent Sendai Framework for Disaster Risk Reduction.[35]

The scientific basis for assessing natural hazards is well established. The National Hazards Research Platform was established and funded in 2009 by the Ministry of Business, Innovation and Employment to support long-term collaborative research on natural hazards, and one of the eleven

National Science Challenges focuses on 'resilience to nature's challenges'. There has been a much greater emphasis in recent years on improving the resilience of communities and the services and infrastructure on which they depend. This has included a variety of initiatives at the sub-national level.[36] Additionally, there are a number of major research projects specifically focused on the impacts and implications of climate change, such as the Deep South Challenge.

Public funds have also been established to anticipate major financial risks and to help pre-fund certain future liabilities. These include: the National Disaster Fund for natural disasters, administered by the Earthquake Commission; the New Zealand Superannuation Fund which is designed to cover part of the cost of future public pension liabilities in the context of an ageing population; and a fund administered by the Accident Compensation Corporation to cover the full lifetime costs of accident claims.

The Christchurch earthquakes proved a severe test of New Zealand's capacities to handle major financial risk. The National Disaster Fund was largely depleted by paid claims of $9 billion, the private insurance sector paid out a further $15 billion, and the government had to meet other liabilities, including the acquisition of unsafe urban land and the estimated $500 million liabilities of an insolvent insurer. Fortunately, these financial stresses did not have significant negative macroeconomic impacts. Indeed, the influx of funds for the recovery and rebuild was a major factor in the buoyancy of the economy during 2012–16.

Against this, critics of current policy settings highlight a number of weaknesses. Amongst these are gaps regarding the anticipatory governance of the risks faced.[37] These include:

- the absence of comprehensive national assessment and reporting on risks;
- the lack of a national risk register;[38]
- the absence of an overall national plan and fund for risk reduction; and
- the lack of regular stress-testing of resilience and adaptive capacity.

Having said this, efforts are currently under way to address some of these deficiencies. For instance, there are moves afoot to add 'the management of significant risks from natural hazards' as a matter of national importance in Section 6 of the Resource Management Act, and initiatives are being taken to replace the Civil Defence Emergency Management Strategy with a more risk-focused National Disaster Resilience Strategy aligned with the Sendai Framework.

Negotiating durable political bargains

If major long-term policy issues are to be tackled, especially those requiring significant non-simultaneous exchanges over lengthy time horizons, then it is highly desirable to secure durable cross-party agreements, at least on the core elements of an effective long-term strategy. Without a broad political consensus, as argued in Chapter 2, there will be at least three risks: firstly, governments may procrastinate and delay taking the measures required to protect long-term interests; secondly, governments may adopt half-hearted and less effective measures; and thirdly, future governments may reverse some or all of the measures implemented by their predecessors, thus undermining the efficacy of the original interventions.

In New Zealand there have been relatively few cases in recent decades of explicit multi-party agreements on major policy issues with significant long-term implications. Perhaps the best example is the deal reached by three parliamentary parties (National, Labour and the Alliance) in 1993 on the structure, coverage and generosity of the country's public pension scheme – New Zealand Superannuation.[39] Attempts to reach similar kinds of formal cross-party agreements on other major long-term issues – whether environmental issues such as climate change mitigation and the management of freshwater resources, or social policy issues like poverty alleviation and welfare reform – have all failed. To date, therefore, the expectation that the introduction of proportional representation in the mid-1990s would create a more consensual political culture and witness the negotiation of more frequent and more durable bargains has not been realised.

Having said this, there have been numerous implicit agreements involving the two major political parties on the overall structure of large-scale reforms designed to enhance or protect long-term interests. Examples include the programme of economic liberalisation in the 1980s and early 1990s, the new framework for public sector management established in the late 1980s, the delegation of responsibility for the implementation of monetary policy to the Reserve Bank in 1989, and the reform of the regulatory framework for resource management, as embodied in the Resource Management Act 1991.

New Zealand is not alone in having a history where formal multi-party agreements on major policy issues are relatively rare. Other parliamentary systems with a Westminster-type heritage, such as Australia and Canada, have a similar legacy. But there are democracies where it is more common for major political parties to reach agreement on important long-term issues.

The Scandinavian democracies, in particular, come to mind.[40] Unsurprisingly, therefore, various researchers have explored the conditions for building cross-party consensus, as well as the potential for particular governance mechanisms and policy-making processes to enhance the prospects for securing durable political bargains.[41] I will return to this matter in Chapter 5. For now, however, it is worth noting that governments have from time to time endorsed multi-stakeholder forums and other deliberative processes as a means of brokering societal agreement on tackling important long-term policy challenges. The Land and Water Forum (2009–) is the best recent example.[42] But thus far such efforts have met with only limited success.

Summary of assessment

The preceding analysis paints a very mixed picture of the quality of anticipatory governance in New Zealand. On the one hand, there are numerous commitment devices, both of a substantive and a procedural nature, that oblige decision-makers at multiple levels of governance to take future-oriented interests into account, adhere to future-focused policy principles, develop long-term plans (e.g. for infrastructure) and report regularly on their performance. There are also various independent public (or quasi-public) institutions that have a mandate to represent specific long-term interests. Without doubt, some of the mechanisms for managing natural hazards, including the National Disaster Fund, have demonstrated their value in the face of significant tests from recent seismic activity.

On the other hand, many of the relevant commitment devices are relatively weak or only partially applied. Requiring policy-makers to be good stewards of resources, take a precautionary approach or pursue the goal of sustainability is one thing; being clear about what such objectives mean in practice and ensuring compliance is quite another. Matters are not helped by the lack of requirements for governments to be explicit about their long-term goals or the intertemporal implications of their policy decisions. Patchy monitoring, weak foresight institutions and unsatisfactory policy frameworks for managing risk, especially the effects of climate change, further reduce the quality of our anticipatory governance. Finally, it is all very well having ambitious long-term goals, such as to eradicate all non-native predators, but if the necessary resources are not allocated and the relevant accountabilities are weak, there is little prospect of success.

ASSESSING POLICY OUTCOMES USING AN ANTICIPATORY LENS

Thus far the focus here has been on New Zealand's current institutional arrangements and policy frameworks and the extent to which they promote anticipatory governance. But what about the *results* of all these arrangements? Are they good, bad or indifferent? And what might current policy outcomes mean for *future* outcomes – whether in 5, 10 or 100 years from now?

In assessing current outcomes through a forward-looking lens we need discernment. Some recent outcomes will affect future prospects much more than others – their impacts, whether positive or negative, will be more widespread or lasting. Relevant criteria include:

- whether recently observed trends are stable, accelerating or decelerating;
- whether there are likely to be cumulative effects, tipping points and non-linear effects;
- whether the expected future effects will be significant in scope and scale; and
- above all, whether the adverse outcomes being experienced or expected are reversible.[43]

Evidence of deteriorating public infrastructure matters. But infrastructure, like roads, drains and electricity grids, can generally be repaired or replaced, albeit at a cost. By contrast, many ecosystems lack such flexibility. Species, once extinct, cannot be resuscitated or resurrected – certainly not on the basis of our current scientific knowledge. Soil erosion, similarly, has permanent and often cumulative impacts. As our oceans acidify, there will be profound consequences for marine life, some of them irreversible. Meanwhile, cleaning up rivers, streams and lakes damaged by excessive inflows of nutrients and sediment or increasing concentrations of pathogens may take many decades – or even longer.[44] Indeed, in some cases it may not be feasible. Likewise, the adverse impacts of childhood poverty can blight a person throughout their adulthood and also affect their offspring in deleterious ways. Hence, high rates of childhood poverty, especially for protracted periods, do not bode well for the future; nor do high rates of childhood obesity. They are no gateway to heaven.

In thinking about outcomes, therefore, we need to prioritise, giving particular attention to results which are likely to have significant, and perhaps irreversible, implications for society's future wellbeing. Additionally, we must reflect on the *drivers* of the outcomes being observed. Are these drivers diminishing or intensifying, and are they likely to contribute to worsening or improving outcomes in the future?

With such considerations in mind, the available

evidence on outcomes in New Zealand yields a mixed assessment.[45] Within specific policy domains, for instance, there are often strikingly divergent results. Take public health: concerted governmental efforts for almost three decades have contributed to a steady reduction in rates of tobacco smoking across all age groups.[46] Rates of adult smoking have roughly halved since the mid-1980s. And New Zealand has set an ambitious 'end game' goal to cut smoking rates to 5 per cent or less by 2025, with strong pricing policies to match. Given the long-term harmful health effects of smoking, these results are positive. They will contribute to better health outcomes in the future. Against this, measures to tackle obesity have been much less concerted and correspondingly less successful. Much the same applies to substance abuse, including alcohol. Nevertheless, rates of potentially hazardous drinking amongst those aged fifteen and older were slightly lower in 2013–14 (at around 18 per cent) than in 2006–07 (at close to 20 per cent).[47]

Outcomes not only diverge significantly within, but also across, policy domains. On the one hand, there are important areas, such as fiscal and monetary policy, where strong commitment devices have been implemented since the late 1980s to protect future-oriented interests (i.e. via the Public Finance Act 1989 and the Reserve Bank

Act 1989). These devices have had a positive impact on policy decisions and outcomes. Over recent decades, for instance, New Zealand has achieved an enviable record with regard to inflation (except for asset prices) and fiscal management – as reflected in the substantial reduction in net public debt since the early 1990s.[48]

On the other hand, in many policy areas outcomes have been much less satisfactory, often with significant intergenerational implications. Some notable examples include:

- relatively high rates of childhood poverty and material deprivation, including limited public investment in mitigating disadvantages experienced during *early* childhood which often have the most lasting negative impacts;[49]
- large gaps in educational achievement on multiple measures between children from different socio-economic and ethnic backgrounds, with limited evidence of improvement over recent decades;[50]
- high and increasing rates of adult and childhood obesity, with almost a third of adults (i.e. those aged fifteen years and over) obese in 2014–15, a further 35 per cent of adults overweight but not obese, and a third of children either obese or overweight;[51]
- poor outcomes with respect to housing, including declining rates of home ownership,

as well as serious problems of overcrowding, homelessness and low-quality private rental accommodation, the product of, amongst other things, inadequate investment in social housing, weak incentives for the construction of low-cost homes and substandard regulation;[52]

- continuing low-density urban development, resulting in the progressive loss of agricultural land and ecosystem services (e.g. carbon sequestration in soils and/or trees), increasing the overall costs of infrastructure, and helping to lock in wasteful patterns of transport energy use, with associated higher carbon emissions (at least in the medium-term);[53]
- significant traffic congestion and detrimental air quality impacts arising from poor traffic management and inadequate investment in public infrastructure, especially in Auckland;[54] and
- weak environmental performance on many important measures, arising in part from poor resource management, insufficient funding of conservation and inadequate protection of certain forms of renewable natural capital (e.g. freshwater).[55]

The picture in relation to environmental outcomes is particularly sobering. For instance:

- New Zealand has one of the world's worst records for the loss of native habitat and biodiversity. For instance, 799 native species were 'threatened' in 2011, of which 417 were in a 'critical' state, 175 'endangered' and 207 'vulnerable'. Overall, 40 per cent of bird species and 85 per cent of native lizards are threatened or at risk.[56] Further, to quote a government report on New Zealand's marine environment in late 2016: 'Most of our marine bird species are threatened with or at risk of extinction, including species of albatrosses, penguins, and herons. More than one-quarter of our marine mammal species are threatened with extinction, including the New Zealand sea lion and species of dolphins and whales.'[57]
- Investment in pest control has been inadequate, with serious efforts to control possums, rats and stoats limited to about one-eighth of the conservation estate.[58] This is contributing to significant ecological damage.
- New Zealand has serious problems of soil erosion, with a rate of soil loss annually about ten times the global average.[59]
- New Zealand has relatively high greenhouse gas emissions per capita (certainly if agricultural emissions are included). Also, despite most of our electricity being generated from renewable resources, our

per capita carbon dioxide emissions are not much different to those of Europe and Japan – which still rely on fossil fuels for a substantial proportion of their stationary energy. New Zealand's ineffective price-based mechanisms and deficient regulatory frameworks have contributed to these unsatisfactory results.[60]

It would be erroneous to imply that policy outcomes in New Zealand are generally poor, whether by the standards of other advanced democracies or more widely. Indeed, there is evidence that on a number of measures relevant for future wellbeing New Zealand performs comparatively well. For instance, our ecological footprint per capita is low by OECD standards, as is our level of government debt per child.[61] Further, the pro-elder bias in social spending appears to be at the low end of the spectrum, at least on one measure.[62]

Nevertheless, there are many outcomes across a range of policy domains which are far from satisfactory. Some of these point to even greater problems in the future, especially in the area of environmental performance. Such outcomes reflect the failure of successive governments to exercise wise stewardship and adopt a sound anticipatory approach. Too often, governments, regardless of their ideological orientations, have been reluctant to make the hard choices necessary in order to deliver better long-term outcomes. Nor have they been willing to invest adequately in enhancing societal understanding about some of the major long-term challenges facing the country or in building support for the reforms necessary to tackle these challenges.

CONCLUSION

Any single lens offers an incomplete picture; it reveals some things but not others. Nevertheless, viewing New Zealand governance arrangements and policy outcomes through an *anticipatory* lens provides grounds for both celebration and lament. On the positive side of the ledger, our institutions and policy settings have numerous strengths: they embody many of the principles, structures, processes and capabilities needed to protect our long-term interests – or at least those interests which a relatively small nation state has the capacity to protect through independent initiatives. Likewise, there are many examples of policy outcomes today which provide hope for even better outcomes tomorrow.

Yet there are also notable weaknesses and worrying trends. New Zealand governments have responded inadequately over recent decades to a number of grave long-term environmental threats, above all climate change. The efforts to decarbonise our economy have been slow, hesitant and vacillating. The attempts to prepare for the impacts of climate change have been equally lacklustre. Whereas we have prepared, at least modestly, for the extra fiscal costs of an ageing population,[63] we have barely begun to think about the massive long-term costs of adapting to climate change. These policy failures are not the result of insufficient information or ignorance about what is at stake. Rather, they reflect deeper pathologies within our democratic institutions, civil society and political culture. Fortunately, some of the problems identified in this chapter can be remedied – albeit partially. Various proposed remedies are outlined in Chapter 5.

5. IMPROVING ANTICIPATORY GOVERNANCE
AN AGENDA FOR REFORM

In our every deliberation, we must consider the impact of our decisions on the next seven generations.
– from The Great Law of the Iroquois Confederacy

An investment in knowledge pays the best interest.
– often attributed to Benjamin Franklin

It is time to investigate possible solutions. How can New Zealand better safeguard the interests of future generations? More specifically, how can governments, in the face of strong short-termist pressures, be better equipped and incentivised to protect long-term interests? What reforms – whether institutional, procedural or regulatory – might increase the likelihood of future risks and vulnerabilities receiving adequate attention and improve policy-making for the long-term common good?

STARTING POINTS

As previous chapters have highlighted, protecting the future involves multiple challenges. These include a lack of attention to creeping policy problems and those with cumulative impacts, a failure to heed credible early warnings or take seriously the costs of inaction, a downplaying of risks and foreseeable harms, a disregard for inconvenient scientific evidence, a devaluing of certain kinds of 'goods', an underinvestment in preventative measures, and a reluctance to impose near-term burdens in order to safeguard long-term interests. Aside from this, technological innovations are occurring at an ever-faster pace, leaving little time to anticipate their impacts, evaluate possible hazards and develop thoughtful, measured policy responses.

Hence, the quest for better anticipatory governance needs to be utterly realistic, yet appropriately ambitious. Improvement is possible, but not perfection. There are no silver bullets or single solutions that will ensure that future interests are properly protected. We do not live in that kind of world. Aside from humanity's inherent faults and failings, we are faced with deep uncertainty, indeterminacy, complexity, contingency, cascading effects, multiple systemic risks and inevitable surprises. In many cases our ratio of knowledge to ignorance is low and our understanding of causality is often poor or contested.

For such reasons, safeguarding the future requires a multi-pronged approach with tailored, cost-effective initiatives across the broad sweep of governmental activity. In fashioning an overall strategy, three preliminary points warrant emphasis.

First, as a general rule it is preferable to build on and strengthen existing institutions, policy frameworks and processes rather than introduce entirely new ones. Amongst other things the former approach is typically cheaper, easier politically and less time-consuming.

Second, a core goal must be to counter the presentist bias in policy-making by shifting the temporal horizon of decision-makers and citizens towards the future. In other words, the long term must be brought into sharper day-to-day political focus. This means finding ways to increase the incentives on decision-makers to take long-term societal interests seriously and reduce their future-oriented attentional deficits. Part of the solution must be to *mainstream* or *embed* a concern for the future within day-to-day policy-making frameworks and processes rather than treating it as an optional extra or expendable luxury.

Third, it is crucial to learn from the past,

including the experience of other countries. And there are many relevant lessons. To take but one: it is sometimes suggested that a good way to protect the future is to have an institution, such as a Commission for the Future, with a broad mission to represent long-term interests. But a commission with a *generalised* responsibility to represent all future interests is unlikely to be effective. Such a task is simply too sweeping, diffuse, imprecise and open-ended. There are, after all, a multiplicity of future interests – as many as there are current interests. No commission, however well resourced, could adequately investigate, let alone represent, all these interests. Moreover, some future interests will be in tension with others: hence, they cannot all be pursued with equal vigour or to the same extent. New Zealand's history lends support to the difficulties facing such an entity. A Commission for the Future with an open-ended mandate was established in 1976 by a National government. But it survived less than a decade and contributed only modestly to policy reform. By contrast, the Parliamentary Commissioner for the Environment, which has a more specific mandate and guaranteed independence, has lasted for three decades and has often been an influential voice for better environmental stewardship.

Several implications follow. Safeguarding the

future requires clarity of purpose, a sharp focus and carefully tailored initiatives. Vague generalities and wishful thinking have no place. Specificity of purpose matters. As Jacqueline McGlade, a former executive director of the European Environment Agency, put it:

if we are to respond more responsibly to the early warning signals of change, we will need to re-design our style of governance to one which reflects a future defined by the local and specific rather than only the global and average.[1]

Likewise, as Steffen Foss Hansen and Joel Tickner emphasise, each risk we face 'is unique, as is the science and politics behind it, and hence a flexible approach is needed, adapted to the nature of the problem'.[2]

Accordingly, if a Commission for the Future were to be (re-)established in New Zealand it would need a clearly prescribed mission, a manageable set of responsibilities and guaranteed independence from the executive. An alternative, and possibly better, approach is to have a series of future-focused institutions with mandates to represent narrower and well-defined interests – whether cultural, economic, environmental, security-related or social. A number of such institutions already exist in New Zealand and could readily be strengthened. Several new ones are recommended below.

SPECIFIC PROPOSALS

The following discussion concentrates on six main ways to improve New Zealand's anticipatory governance:

1. protecting and enhancing our democratic institutions through constitutional reform;
2. embedding the future more deeply within our democratic institutions and policy processes through the use of various kinds of commitment devices;
3. enhancing the political system's capacity for foresight, including the ability to detect the emergent;
4. strengthening institutional voices for the future, including the stewardship responsibilities of the public service;
5. embedding the future within policy frameworks; and
6. nurturing a future-focused political culture that facilitates durable political bargains on important intergenerational issues.

The various proposals under each topic are summarised in Table 5.1.

Three caveats deserve mention before proceeding. First, space permits only a brief sketch of the kinds of reforms that deserve consideration. On each topic, a great deal more could be said. In most cases, the relevant analysis is available elsewhere.³ For others, it still needs to be written!

Second, the focus here is on domestic policy issues rather than global ones. Also, no specific attention is given to safeguarding the future in relation to matters of defence, intelligence, cyber-security, terrorism or related topics. Such issues deserve separate consideration.

Third, most of the proposals advanced below concentrate on tackling the presentist bias in policy-making through the lever of *institutional* reform. They do not deal with the many detailed *policy* changes required in specific areas of governmental activity to address the numerous long-term problems mentioned in previous chapters, such as population ageing, the obesity pandemic or coping with disruptive technologies. But the proposed institutional reforms can be expected to incentivise and assist governments to implement the required policy responses – in part by enhancing the transparency, responsiveness and accountability of our democratic institutions and improving the quality of the information with which citizens can assess governmental effectiveness.

Given the importance of better environmental stewardship for the wellbeing of future generations, the chapter concludes with some specific suggestions for strengthening environmental governance, particularly in relation to climate

Table 5.1 Ways to enhance anticipatory governance in New Zealand – summary

Type of reform	Specific proposals
Constitutional reform	Extend the parliamentary term to four years.
	Incorporate specific environmental rights into the Bill of Rights Act.
	Consider a written, entrenched constitution, including specific protections for future generations.
Improve long-term reporting	Implement a Social Reporting Act requiring, at a minimum, periodic reporting of all major social outcomes and their long-term societal and policy implications.
	Implement a Long-Term Reporting Act requiring governments to produce periodic intergenerational reports.
	Implement a Risk Reporting Act requiring governments to report annually on major risks and recent losses, including trends in disaster risk, progress on disaster risk reduction and proposed policy changes.
	Include provisions in the Public Finance Act requiring the governments to prepare a report responding to the findings of the Treasury's Long-Term Fiscal Statement.
	Require major reports on policy outcomes and trends to include commentaries on the significance and long-term implications of the findings.
	Require regular reports on progress towards meeting long-term policy targets, including the UN Sustainable Development Goals.
	Require regular reporting on the intergenerational fairness of current policies.
Improve foresight capability	Establish a dedicated foresight unit in a central agency.
	Establish a parliamentary select committee for the future.
Strengthen future-focused institutions	Enhance the stewardship role of the public service (e.g. by placing briefings to incoming ministers on a statutory basis and including a section on foresight).
	Enhance the role of evidence in the policy-making process (e.g. by placing the role of the Prime Minister's Chief Science Advisor on a statutory basis).
	Enhance the resources available to existing future-focused institutions, such as the Parliamentary Commissioner for the Environment.

Type of reform	Specific proposals
Embed the future within policy frameworks	Apply lower discount rates in cost-benefit analyses, especially for periods exceeding thirty years and when there are risks of catastrophic or irreversible consequences.
	Develop an intergenerational fairness index or a series of domain-specific indices.
	Enhance the specifications of the Treasury's Living Standards Framework (e.g. regarding equity and sustainability).
	Develop and report measures of comprehensive wealth.
	Give greater weight to path dependence and irreversibility in policy analysis and decision-making.
	Develop statutory guidelines for the application of the precautionary principle.
Nurture a future-focused political culture	Enhance deliberative mechanisms for decision-making.
	Enhance political trust, in part by reducing income and wealth inequality.
Improve environmental stewardship and adaptive governance	More comprehensive and cost-effective measures to minimise negative environmental externalities.
	Establish new institutions to strengthen the capacity to mitigate and adapt to climate change.

change. To quote Jan Wright, the Parliamentary Commissioner for the Environment: 'The need for forward thinking is crucial when it comes to the most serious environmental issue of all – climate change – where the future is so much more important than the past.'[4]

1. CONSTITUTIONAL REFORM

Robust democratic institutions are vital for good governance, not least anticipatory governance. Protecting the vitality and resilience of these institutions is thus essential if citizens' long-term interests – across the full sweep of policy domains – are to be properly safeguarded.

There are grounds for concern about New Zealand's current constitutional arrangements. As Sir Geoffrey Palmer and Andrew Butler have recently argued: 'Our constitution is not fully fit for purpose.'[5] It is, in their view: 'dangerously incomplete, obscure, fragmentary and far too flexible. It remorselessly evolves with political developments and is subject to few limits. It evolves in obscure and unpredictable ways that are not transparent.'[6]

To address these concerns, they propose that New Zealand implement a proper, written, codified constitution. They also recommend several important constitutional reforms, one of which has the potential to improve the quality of legislation and enhance the capacity of governments to address complex, long-term problems – namely an extension of the current three-year parliamentary term to four years.

This is not the place for a detailed exploration of the pros and cons of a written, entrenched constitution. But the ideas advanced by Sir Geoffrey Palmer and Andrew Butler deserve very careful attention and rigorous public debate. We need to take our constitutional arrangements seriously and assess the options for improvement. In particular, there is a strong case for a fixed, four-year term

– as, for instance, is common in Europe.[7] On its own, of course, such a reform would not extend the time horizons of governments greatly and would certainly not overcome the presentist bias in policy-making. But it would be a good place to start. The main challenge would be to convince the public of the case for extending the term and making it fixed (or at least semi-fixed).[8] There have already been two referenda during the past half century on increasing the term of Parliament to four years – and both were heavily defeated. There would be little point holding a further referendum unless there was a reasonable chance of success. Yet such success may hinge on whether voters are convinced that our democratic institutions are sufficiently transparent, responsive and accountable. In the absence of the kinds of reforms outlined below, this is likely to be more difficult.

A fiscal constitution?

In recent decades there have been many proposals for democracies like New Zealand to protect the interests of future generations by means of a fiscal constitution. The aim of such constitutions is to enshrine particular fiscal rules in a country's fundamental laws (where these exist) in order to make it more difficult for governments to run large deficits and accumulate substantial public debt. For fiscal conservatives, such as the late James

Buchanan (a Nobel laureate in economics), another goal is to constrain the size and role of the state, for instance by limiting tax rates and/or the level of public expenditure beyond specified thresholds.[9] But fiscal rules can be crafted in multiple ways, and there are many possible approaches that would not necessarily curb public expenditure. For instance, the economist Antonio Rangel has proposed a fiscal rule that would require governments to spend a minimum amount on 'forward intergenerational goods' for every dollar spent on the elderly (or 'backward intergenerational goods').[10]

While fiscal constitutions have certain attractions, they pose formidable challenges with respect to design and implementation – not least the problem of securing the necessary political agreement on their wording. They also run the risk of generating excessive policy rigidity and unduly constraining governmental responses to economic crises, natural disasters and threats to national security. In New Zealand's case, the scope for a fiscal constitution is limited by the absence of a written, entrenched constitution (as noted earlier). Moreover, the principles of fiscal responsibility embodied in the Public Finance Act currently provide a useful, and thus far relatively effective, mechanism for protecting the fiscal interests of future generations. While there is no pressing need to modify them, there are several other policy changes that could be made to enhance the country's long-term fiscal management, as argued below. There is also a good case, as recommended by Transparency International New Zealand several years ago, for increasing the level of fiscal transparency and accountability (e.g. by enhancing various aspects of fiscal reporting, such as data on tax expenditures, and giving Parliament greater access to independent advice on important fiscal issues).[11]

2. COMMITTING TO A BETTER FUTURE

As discussed in Chapter 4, New Zealand already has a significant number of commitment devices that are designed, at least in part, to protect the future and enhance the quality of anticipatory governance. But some of the existing devices are weak (e.g. they lack a statutory basis) and the current framework contains important gaps.

The aim of a commitment device – whether in the form of a marriage vow, a policy target, a multi-party agreement or a legal requirement for governments to abide by procedural rules or substantive principles – is to bind a person, organisation or government to a particular course of action or to conform to specified norms.[12] Such devices operate by limiting future discretion or reinforcing self-restraint. In particular, they penalise bad behaviour, like reneging, defecting or taking easy options. In this way, they can reduce the propensity for actions considered impatient, impulsive, expedient, myopic or narrowly self-interested. Importantly, this can affect the intertemporal payoff structure, rebalancing the scales to protect long-term interests.

Potentially, there are many other commitment devices, of both a procedural and substantive kind, that could be added to the current stock and that might help to safeguard future interests. But some of the possibilities are much harder to implement than others. For instance, if New Zealand had a written constitution with the status of supreme law, specific provisions could be incorporated to protect future generations – such as a right to an 'ecologically healthy environment' or an environment that is 'not harmful' to a person's 'health or wellbeing'.[13] But a constitutional commitment device of this kind is not currently feasible – and may not be for a long time (if ever). An alternative approach would be to incorporate within the Bill of Rights Act (1990) a new provision protecting specific future-oriented rights, such as environmental rights.[14] It would be important, however, to word such a provision carefully to ensure that it was likely to afford additional protection. Note, too, that provisions in the Bill of Rights Act can readily be altered or overridden by Parliament. Hence, any new provision relating to environmental rights, however framed, has only a limited capacity to safeguard future interests.

Aside from commitment devices of a constitutional (or quasi-constitutional) nature, there are many non-constitutional measuwres that could be implemented with relatively little difficulty and for only a modest cost. Here are some suggestions.

Strengthening existing commitment devices
Various existing commitment devices could be strengthened. Take, for instance, the requirement for the Treasury to produce a long-term fiscal statement. Currently, although Parliament's Finance and Expenditure Committee scrutinises these documents, there is no statutory obligation for the government to respond to the Treasury's findings – for example, by indicating how it plans to address any significant long-term fiscal challenges which have been highlighted. If such a requirement were added, governments would need to be more transparent about their long-term intentions and give greater thought to the management of long-term fiscal risks. Accountability would also be enhanced if responsibility for chairing the Finance and Expenditure Committee were to reside with an Opposition MP – as, for instance, is the case with the Public Accounts Committee of the British House of Commons.

Further, the Parliamentary Commissioner for the Environment has recently recommended that each of the domain and synthesis reports on the environment produced jointly by the Ministry for the Environment and Statistics New Zealand should provide a commentary at the end dealing with the outlook for different environmental issues.[15] In some cases this might include quantitative projections and risk assessments. As the Commissioner, Dr Jan Wright, has observed:

We need both evidence and reasoning to be able to judge which environmental issues we should worry about the most. We also need to know which environmental issues we should worry about the least – and which we should worry about somewhat. We need perspective on the state of our environment. ... The significance of an environmental issue cannot be judged without looking ahead. If the pressures that are damaging an aspect of the environment are expected to decrease, then there may be less reason for concern. If significant policy and regulation changes have been put in place to address the issue, again there may be less reason for concern. But if a tipping point is approaching or the scale of the problem is accelerating, there will be more reason for concern. ... The need for forward thinking is crucial when it comes to the most serious environmental issue of all – climate change – where the future is so much more important than the past. For instance, it is very important to convey to the reader that the sea will continue to rise for centuries to come even if global greenhouse gas emissions stopped tomorrow.[16]

A similar requirement for forward thinking – that is, to reflect on the future significance of current policy outcomes and trends – could readily be extended and applied to many other regular governmental reports. Indeed, such an approach would be thoroughly consistent with the new provisions in the State Sector Act for departmental chief executives to exercise 'stewardship' responsibilities (as noted in Chapter 4). To be sure, there would be a fiscal cost. There would also be a risk of such commentaries being written in highly generalised terms. Nevertheless, requirements of this nature would increase the likelihood of government agencies and their respective ministers looking beyond their immediate horizons and thinking more carefully about the long-term implications of current policy settings.

Creating new commitment devices
Just as there is a case for strengthening some existing commitment devices, there are equally grounds for adding new ones. Here are three suggestions.

A) A Social Reporting (or Social Responsibility) Act. While there are currently statutory requirements for regular and comprehensive fiscal and environmental reporting, there are no similar legislative provisions with respect to social issues and outcomes (e.g. covering objective and subjective wellbeing, standards of living, income and wealth distribution, health, housing, paid work, knowledge and skills, cultural identity, and crime and punishment). Of course, many departments and agencies, such as the Ministries of Education, Health, Justice and Social Development, publish large numbers of reports – many of them annually – on all manner of policy or research-related issues. But comprehensive social reporting lacks a firm statutory basis.

A Social Responsibility Act, potentially modelled on the provisions in the Public Finance Act relating to fiscal responsibility, has been advocated since the mid-1990s.[17] During the 2000s, after much debate amongst government officials, a modified and scaled-down version of such a statute – in the form of a Social Reporting Act – was recommended to the government by the Ministry of Social Development. As the name suggests, the proposed Act focused on regular *social reporting* rather than a broader conception of *social responsibility*. But to date, for reasons that are not entirely clear, no government has been willing to take even this modest step.

To compound matters, the National-led government has placed little weight on social reporting since taking office in late 2008. As a result, although the Ministry of Social Development produced Social Reports annually between 2001 and 2010, there was a six-year break until the next one was published in 2016. Unfortunately, the continuing lack of ministerial interest in such reporting looks set to ensure that the 2016 document will be the last, at least for a while.

Placing Social Reports on a firm statutory basis would reduce the risk of their regular publication being at the mercy of narrow political factors or fluctuating ministerial priorities. As for other documents of a similar kind, all future Social Reports should include a section commenting on the significance of the outcomes reported, especially their *long-term* societal and policy implications. Such a section could also contain a distributional analysis of government social expenditures, including how particular age groups or cohorts fare.[18]

Aside from requiring regular reporting and analysis of social outcomes, legislation could go further and impose obligations on governments to act in accordance with specified principles of social responsibility – in the same way that the Public Finance Act requires governments to exercise proper fiscal responsibility. Under a Social Responsibility Act of this kind a range of principles could be enunciated, for example:

- ensuring that all citizens are able to satisfy their basic needs (e.g. food, clothing, shelter, education and health care);

- minimising rates of material hardship and income-based poverty;
- adequately protecting citizens' health and safety in the workplace;
- adequately protecting society's least advantaged and most vulnerable citizens (e.g. children, the elderly and disabled); and
- acting consistently with the requirements of intergenerational fairness.

Admittedly, incorporating principles of this nature into legislation – whether via a Social Responsibility Act or another instrument – is open to a variety of philosophical and practical objections.[19] It is not possible to explore these here. But it is disappointing that such matters have thus far received so little public attention. It is incumbent on any society that aspires to be *good* and *just* to ensure that the basic social needs of its citizens are adequately satisfied, that their social rights are properly protected and that considerations of intergenerational fairness are given due weight in policy-making. New Zealand has been falling short of meeting these tests for far too long.

B) A Long-Term Reporting Act. A separate and complementary approach would be to enact a Long-Term Reporting Act. Such a statute could cover the following matters: periodic intergenerational reports; reporting on intergenerational fairness; and reporting progress towards meeting long-term policy targets.

To turn to the first possible function of a Long-Term Reporting Act: governments could be legally obliged to produce every second parliamentary term (or at least once every eight years assuming a four-year term) a substantive report on the future.[20] This could be called an 'Intergenerational Report' or a 'Government Statement on Long-Term Issues'. Unlike the Long-Term Fiscal Statement it would be the responsibility of the Cabinet, not the Treasury; it would thus be a ministerial document. It would also be somewhat broader in scope, with a longer time horizon.

While the precise contents of such reports should be a matter for each government to determine, the relevant statute could be written so as to ensure that they cover significant issues and encourage serious reflection on long-term risks and opportunities. The aim, in other words, would be to embody the characteristics of good anticipatory governance. To illustrate, the legislation could specify that each report must, *inter alia*:

1. consider a time horizon of at least a hundred years;
2. provide an overall assessment of the major long-term risks, both natural and man-made, facing the country;

3. identify the trends and signals that are particularly concerning for future wellbeing, including societal and cultural trends (e.g. issues of family structure, demography, social cohesion, inclusion, alienation, identity and diversity), major natural hazards and evolving climate change risks;

4. evaluate the government's risk management capability and adaptive capacity;

5. evaluate progress towards achieving important long-term governmental targets, including those embodied in international agreements (e.g. the United Nations Sustainable Development Goals and climate change treaties);[21]

6. review the long-term economic, social and environmental implications of, and possible ways of addressing, at least one slow-onset problem and/or a problem which is likely to have significant cumulative effects;

7. evaluate the economic, social and environmental implications of at least one large-scale emerging technology; and

8. set new or additional measurable and meaningful goals to address at least one long-term policy problem.

Additionally, there could be a statutory requirement for the government to seek expert advice, including from the Royal Society of New Zealand, in preparing each report. There should also be mandated opportunities for public consultation and input during the process, as for instance occurs during the preparation of the government's periodic long-term reports in Finland.[22] To ensure high-level political engagement, responsibility for such reports should rest with the Prime Minister. Further, under Parliament's Standing Orders there should be a requirement for intergenerational reports to be scrutinised by a select committee (see below), with an opportunity for public submissions and open public hearings, and subsequently debated in the House.

A Long-Term Reporting Act could also oblige governments to report more regularly and fully on the intergenerational implications of their policy decisions, particularly those with major long-term ramifications. This could include the development of an index of intergenerational fairness – or perhaps more realistically and appropriately, separate indices within different policy domains.[23] Such reporting would provide greater transparency regarding the intertemporal implications of current policy settings and proposed changes.

Finally, a Long-Term Reporting Act could further mandate the reporting of *progress* towards meeting long-term policy targets. The setting of policy targets is already a widely used commitment device. Such targets serve multiple purposes:

they signal direction, focus attention, harness bureaucratic effort and enhance accountability. But there is a risk, especially when targets are long-term (e.g. ten years or more), that they will lack political salience. Governments may also prefer to downplay particular targets, all the more so if performance towards meeting them is unsatisfactory. For instance, the government set a target in 2011 to reduce New Zealand's greenhouse gas emissions by 2050 by 50 per cent compared to 1990 levels. But since then the target has rarely been referred to by ministers. No doubt this is partly because emissions have not been tracking towards meeting the target and because the government has lacked an effective strategy to achieve its stated long-term objective.[24]

One option for strengthening the political salience of policy targets would be to make it mandatory for governments to set specific and meaningful milestones whenever they establish formal targets extending beyond, say, five years or ten years. Take, for instance, the ambitious target to make New Zealand predator free within 35 years: several milestones have been set for 2025, including the suppression or removal of pests from an additional one million hectares, demonstrating that predator-free areas can be created without the use of fences and eliminating all introduced predators from offshore island nature reserves.

While milestones of this nature are positive, the government has thus far committed only modest public resources to the predator-free goal. Without adequate long-term funding, the project will struggle to gain traction.

Another option would be to make it mandatory for governments to publish an annual report which records all their publicly announced targets across the full sweep of policy domains and assesses progress towards meeting them. Where progress is inadequate, there could be a requirement for the government to state what remedial actions it will take. Such reports would need to include any targets contained within international agreements, such as those embodied within the Sustainable Development Goals.

Admittedly, there is a risk that statutory reporting requirements of the kind suggested above might discourage governments from setting long-term targets (or sufficiently demanding targets) because of the additional accountability associated with a failure to deliver.[25] There is also a risk that any reporting of progress (or a lack thereof) will be perfunctory. But a failure to set targets or report adequately will expose a government to criticism. Moreover, a suitably framed Long-Term Reporting Act, with appropriate opportunities for public consultation and engagement, might help strengthen public expectations – and hence political incentives – that governments should set ambitious long-term targets and report progress regularly, comprehensively and accurately. And a public expectation of meaningful targets and reliable reporting on progress could encourage more robust policy advice and more prudent, forward-looking policy formulation. In such an environment, governments which fail to meet public expectations will risk criticism that they lack a proper concern for the future. Whether such criticism is electorally damaging will depend, amongst other things, on the strength of the political community's commitment to future-focused values.

C) A Risk Reporting Act. In addition to the requirement for reporting on major long-term risks via periodic intergenerational reports, there is a case for enacting legislation that obliges governments to prepare an annual report to Parliament on risk management. Such a report should cover the major risks facing New Zealand across all relevant policy domains. More specifically, the report should include:

- any changes to the national risk register;
- significant losses due to natural or man-made disasters during the previous year, and the main policy lessons arising from these disasters;

- significant trends in disaster risk;
- progress on disaster risk reduction, including a summary of the results of recent stress tests; and
- any proposed policy changes to mitigate or manage specific risks, including emerging ones.

Such reports should be reviewed by an appropriate parliamentary select committee (possibly the proposed committee on the future – see below), and subsequently debated in the House.

3. IMPROVING THE CAPACITY FOR FORESIGHT

By comparison with many other democracies, including small ones, New Zealand invests relatively little in formal foresight processes and reviews. We have no dedicated, high-level foresight unit in central government, no academic research centre devoted to foresight methodologies and assessments, no national scenarios to use in such assessments, no parliamentary committee focused on emerging and long-term policy issues, few serious evaluations of the societal impacts of emerging technologies[26] and important scientific discoveries, and only sporadic efforts by major departments and agencies to undertake horizon-scanning and scenario analyses in their respective areas of responsibility. A stronger investment in foresight cannot ensure that all future hazards are anticipated or assessed; nor can it guarantee that policy decisions will be more farsighted – in the sense that they better advance the long-term public interest. But it can certainly increase the capacity to identify significant risks and opportunities, including the early detection of harmful trends and developments. Equally, it can help embed disciplined thinking about future consequences in the policy process and counter short-termist tendencies.

There is a strong case for strengthening the foresight capacity of both our executive and legislative institutions. In doing so, we can draw on a wealth of overseas experience. There are many different models. But whatever approach we adopt, the new entities need clear mandates and adequate resources, and must be properly integrated into wider governmental and parliamentary processes.

A dedicated foresight unit in central government
At a minimum, there should be a permanent foresight unit established within one of our three central agencies. Probably the best location is the Department of Prime Minister and Cabinet as this will enhance the prospect of high-level political interest and bureaucratic influence. Ideally, the unit should have a statutory basis. Its functions could be modelled on the activities of the Foresight

and Horizon Scanning teams in the Government Office for Science in London.[27] Under this approach, the unit would be responsible for undertaking in-depth analyses of complex, long-term problems and provide strategic options for policy reform. It would also coordinate the foresight activities of government departments and agencies, provide advice and technical assistance, draw on the resources of the country's universities and other research institutions, and bring emerging issues to the attention of the government and the wider public. It could also be charged with evaluating the impacts of large-scale emerging technologies and assisting the Prime Minister to produce periodic reports on the future.

A parliamentary select committee for the future
There are several structural options for enhancing the quality and depth of legislative foresight and improving parliamentary oversight of governmental efforts to safeguard the future.

The first is to establish a permanent select committee under Parliament's Standing Orders with a specific mandate to focus on future-oriented issues. Such a committee could be modelled on the successful Committee for the Future in the Finnish parliament which was created in 1993.[28] Ideally, it should be chaired by an Opposition MP.

To work effectively, such a committee would

need clearly defined responsibilities. These could include:

1. assessing the quality and implications of the foresight work undertaken by government departments and agencies;
2. reviewing the government's periodic reports on the future and the quality of its intergenerational reporting;
3. scrutinising the performance of government departments in undertaking their 'stewardship' responsibilities under the State Sector Act, including their capacity to address the long-term issues identified in their (triennial) briefings to incoming ministers;
4. reviewing the intergenerational implications of current policy settings;
5. conducting inquiries into the management of creeping issues and other issues with significant long-term implications;
6. assessing the economic, social and environmental implications of important new and emerging technologies;
7. conducting periodic assessments of significant risks, including systemic risks, and emergent economic, social and environmental phenomena;
8. undertaking horizon-scanning exercises; and
9. investigating ways of improving anticipatory governance.

Having a dedicated select committee of this nature would not only bring important long-term policy issues under a parliamentary spotlight, but it would also expose MPs to a range of evidence, methodologies and investigative techniques that are often ignored or poorly understood, such as the assessment of risk. Further, it would enable a more concerted and in-depth consideration of major intertemporal issues – including questions of intergenerational justice – than is normally possible under current parliamentary processes. As part of its remit, a parliamentary committee for the future could be charged with engaging periodically with the public and encouraging wider debate on societal goals and aspirations.

A second option would be to follow the recent practice in Scotland. Here a new institution – in the form of a company – has been established known as Scotland's Futures Forum.[29] It is governed by a board of directors which comprises members of the Scottish parliament and people from various sectors of the community including business and research. It is designed to help parliamentarians and the wider Scottish community assess the long-term challenges facing Scotland and debate ways of better preparing for the future. To this end, it commissions in-depth studies, undertakes scenario-planning, and organises lectures, seminars and workshops on issues of strategic importance. A core objective is to facilitate and encourage non-partisan debate on future-focused issues, not least the kind of society which citizens aspire to build.

A third option would be to require each of Parliament's thirteen subject-oriented select committees to undertake specific foresight work in their respective areas of policy responsibility. A potential advantage of this approach is that it would 'mainstream' such activities across the select committee system. But the likely disadvantage is that investigations of long-term, emerging and creeping problems would receive low priority, as is currently the case.

Of the three options, the first is probably preferable. But there is no reason why a dedicated select committee for the future could not facilitate wider public engagement in a manner similar to that of Scotland's Futures Forum. Indeed, there would be nothing in principle to prevent Parliament from establishing a separate futures forum as part of a wider set of initiatives to enhance the quality of New Zealand's anticipatory governance. It would be important, however, to avoid duplication of effort. If there were to be both a select committee for the future and a futures forum, the purpose and responsibilities of the two entities would need to be clearly differentiated.

4. STRENGTHENING INSTITUTIONAL VOICES FOR THE FUTURE

One of the perennial challenges in protecting long-term interests is that the voice of the present often drowns out the voice of the future. While there is no complete solution to this problem, part of the answer must be to strengthen those institutions whose role is to speak for future-oriented interests, such as the Parliamentary Commissioner for the Environment, the Children's Commissioner and the Retirement Commissioner. As it stands, such institutions are small and very modestly funded. Additional capability would strengthen their roles.

Of all our institutions with responsibilities to think about, and help protect, the long-term public interest, two are pivotal: the public service and our research institutions, especially universities.

THE STEWARDSHIP ROLE OF THE PUBLIC SERVICE

Within a parliamentary democracy like New Zealand, a permanent, professional, non-partisan public service constitutes a large, enduring, future-focused commitment device. While faithfully serving the government of the day, it must also retain the capacity to serve future governments – in perpetuity. By virtue of its statutory roles and ethical norms, the public service helps to ensure that ministers govern in accordance with constitutional conventions and well-established procedures. One way of doing so is by providing ministers – whether they are receptive or otherwise – with free and frank advice. Through strong, evidence-informed independent advice it can discourage opportunistic decision-making and protect the government's interests as an owner, investor and risk bearer (or what is sometimes called the 'ownership interest'). Likewise, during times of political uncertainty it can help to navigate and stabilise the 'ship of state'. The important contribution of the public service to the protection of long-term interests was highlighted in August 2015 by the then Prime Minister, John Key. When launching the 'Policy Project' frameworks – which are designed to improve policy capability and the quality of policy advice – he commented:

it's important that departments invest in long term thinking. ... We need creative thinkers who will challenge us out of status quo thinking and encourage us to take risks in the interests of better long term outcomes. ... Great advice from officials helps ministers balance the needs of today with longer term goals so we can govern better for future generations as well as today. ... While I hold ministers to account for delivering on the priorities of today, they also have a responsibility to ensure their departments are thinking about the challenges of tomorrow. I expect ministers to engage constructively with their chief executives in making space for longer term thinking.

... Ministers and CEs need to balance current priorities with the investment in research, analysis and the deep subject matter expertise and capability needed to provide robust advice about future risks and opportunities.[30]

There has been ongoing debate in New Zealand as to whether departments are sufficiently brave regarding the nature of the policy advice they offer ministers and whether they devote sufficient time to long-term issues.[31] Whatever the strengths and weaknesses of existing practices, there is almost certainly room for improvement, especially given the number of current, as well as emerging, complex societal issues. The new statutory focus on stewardship provides an important lever towards this end. But it needs to be actively engaged. This requires concerted leadership by the State Services Commissioner, Peter Hughes, in fulfilling his statutory responsibility for 'promoting a culture of stewardship in the State services' (to quote Section 4A(i) of the State Sector Act) and strong incentives for departmental chief executives, via their performance agreements and accountability mechanisms, to exercise their stewardship responsibilities (i.e. financial, organisational, regulatory, and so on). In effect, this means embedding the notion of stewardship firmly within all relevant departmental performance management systems. Currently these include:

Statements of Intent, four-year plans, output plans, annual reports and other strategic, monitoring and reporting mechanisms; the Performance Improvement Framework for reviewing departmental performance; the talent management system across the public sector; mechanisms for encouraging system stewardship; and individual performance agreements – beginning with senior managers and cascading down the various 'chains of command'. In some cases, too, additional public funding will be needed to build analytical capacity and strengthen the level and quality of investment in long-term thinking and future-focused policy research.

One specific improvement would be for departments to make better use of the opportunity afforded by their briefings to incoming ministers after each general election. Such briefings could include a more detailed foresight section (with a proper scan of the horizon over coming decades), identify critical long-term issues, and offer strategic advice on ways to address them. To undertake such reporting in a cost-effective way, the more strategic and systemic aspects of such briefings could be led by the central agencies and/or the main sector groupings (e.g. justice, natural resources, social, and so on. Another possibility would be to place the requirement for briefings to incoming ministers on a firm statutory footing (e.g. via the State Sector

Act), with the nature of their coverage (including the scanning of important long-term issues) clearly specified.

The contribution of the Policy Project co-ordinated in recent years by the Department of Prime Minister and Cabinet is highly relevant in this context.[32] Each of the three frameworks which comprise the main outputs of the project thus far place a strong emphasis on stewardship, long-term thinking and/or strategic thinking. The three frameworks cover policy capability, policy skills and policy quality, and are designed to increase the ability of government departments and agencies to provide ministers with the best possible advice on a sustainable basis. It remains to be seen, however, what impact the Policy Project will have on the nature and temporal focus of officials' advice-giving and the quality of the regulatory stewardship exercised by public bodies.

Enhancing the influence of evidence in policy-making

The findings from research and policy evaluation are vital ingredients for ensuring that policy decisions are evidence-informed and forward-looking. Research institutions, especially universities and Crown Research Institutes, are critical to this process. They also play a pivotal role in alerting governments and the public to impending problems and emerging hazards. To perform these functions well, such institutions must be properly funded. Important too, however, is the willingness of researchers to speak out and bring inconvenient truths to the attention of policy-makers. As Shaun Hendy contends: 'Science that is not heard is not science at all.'[33] Unfortunately, there is evidence that not all is well with the transmission of scientific knowledge in New Zealand, with many scientists reluctant to, and sometimes prevented from, contributing to public debate on significant policy issues within their field of expertise. Matters are often not helped by various commercial sensitivities and constraints, the limited pool of experts in New Zealand in particular scientific disciplines (or sub-disciplines), and the fact that scientists within Crown Research Institutes lack the statutory independence afforded to their counterparts in universities.

There are at least two possible ways forward. The first would be to strengthen the resources and mandate of the Prime Minister's Chief Science Advisor, a position currently held by the distinguished paediatrician Sir Peter Gluckman. This could include placing Sir Peter's role on a statutory basis and possibly creating a separate entity external to the Department of Prime Minister and Cabinet but still reporting directly to the Prime Minister.

A second option, as recommended by Professor Hendy, would be to establish a Parliamentary Commission (or Commissioner) for Science, modelled on the Parliamentary Commissioner for the Environment. Such a commission would have wide-ranging investigative powers, explore scientific issues of long-term significance for New Zealand, and serve as an 'honest broker' in the science system.[34] Hendy's proposal wants serious consideration. It would be important, however, to specify the roles of any such commission clearly and avoid undue overlap with the functions of the Royal Society and the Prime Minister's Chief Science Advisor. Amongst other things, such a commission could be charged with reporting to Parliament on:

1. any significant gaps in current research on new and emerging hazards and long-term risks, and how such gaps might be addressed;
2. the extent to which government agencies are making the best possible use of scientific evidence in the advice they provide to governments;
3. any cases of important research findings not being reported publicly in a timely manner, perhaps because of the influence of commercial interests; and
4. the extent to which the precautionary principle is being applied by governments

(or government agencies) in a prudent, consistent and justifiable manner.

5. EMBEDDING THE FUTURE WITHIN POLICY FRAMEWORKS

In many respects, the future is already deeply embedded in the policy frameworks, analytical techniques, management systems and accounting practices employed by governments and their advisers. But there are notable weaknesses with existing arrangements (see Chapter 4). Important changes are thus needed. Here are a few suggestions.

Discounting the future

The discount rate employed in policy analysis has a fundamental impact on how the future is valued. In New Zealand, the Treasury provides guidance to government agencies on conducting cost–benefit analyses.[35] As part of this advice it recommends discount rates for different types of projects or investments, with these rates varying depending on the level of risk and other relevant considerations. Over the years the Treasury has gradually reduced the rates recommended. As of late 2016, the real discount rate recommended varies between 4 per cent for general purpose offices and buildings to 7 per cent for telecommunications, media and technology, IT and equipment, and research and development, with a default rate of 6 per cent for projects that are hard to categorise, including regulatory proposals. While such rates place a greater value on long-term costs and benefits than was previously the case (e.g. when the recommended rates were 8 per cent or higher), they are still higher than those adopted in some comparable jurisdictions. The British Treasury, for instance, recommends a real discount rate of 3.5 per cent.[36] It also favours a declining long-term discount rate (e.g. for periods beyond thirty years), and recommends the use of a lower discount rate when the merits of a project or proposal are materially impacted by the discounting of effects over the very long run.

There is no agreement amongst economists, philosophers and others on the appropriate discount rate. And in my view there is no 'correct' rate. But there are powerful ethical grounds for applying an extremely low discount rate when there is a risk of catastrophic impacts and/or the potential for significant irreversible consequences.[37] There is also a strong case for applying a range of discount rates when assessing, and comparing, the merits of major projects and other policy investments. Sensitivity analyses of this nature will highlight how the discount rate chosen affects the rate of return and enables policy-makers to take such considerations into account. In this regard, it is pleasing that the New Zealand Treasury since 2015 has recommended the use of two different rates when undertaking cost–benefit analyses as part of the budget round. For the 2016 budget the recommended rates were 8 per cent and 4 per cent; for the 2017 budget they were 6 per cent and 3 per cent.[38]

Aside from the issue of discounting, it is important to note that a range of analytical tools have been developed over recent decades for assessing policies and projects with long lifetimes, including those which have the potential to create significant path dependence (such as long-term infrastructure). Some of these tools are specifically designed for situations involving dynamic change and deep uncertainty.[39]

Improving the Treasury's Living Standards Framework

The Treasury's Living Standards Framework (LSF) represents a valuable and important step towards developing a more holistic – and future-focused – approach to policy analysis, one which encompasses the full range of capital stocks and policy impacts. But in its current form it lacks sufficient specification to provide clear guidance to policy-makers. In part this is because some of the five goals to which the LSF gives priority are inadequately stipulated. Take, for instance, the goal of *equity*: the LSF rightly identifies some of the material principles of justice (e.g. equal treatment, the satisfaction of needs, rewarding people for their contribution or effort, etc.) that are relevant for assessing the fairness of policy proposals. It also highlights, appropriately, the broad scope of the domain of justice. But it does not cover the full range of formal and material principles that warrant consideration; nor does it provide criteria for determining priorities if and when such principles conflict. Equally, it supplies little guidance on the meaning of, or requirements for, intergenerational justice. Similar weaknesses are evident in its approach to *sustainability*. The LSF does not grapple in any detail with the debates over the meaning of sustainability, the requirements for its realisation or the related issues of substitutability, biophysical limits and resilience. A good deal more conceptual and ethical clarity will be required before the LSF can be properly and meaningfully operationalised.

Valuing nature and moving towards comprehensive wealth accounting
Another challenge facing the development and application of holistic analytical approaches like the Living Standards Framework is the current lack of data regarding the country's 'comprehensive wealth' or 'inclusive wealth' – that is, our national wealth broadly understood and incorporating most or all capital stocks.[40] Existing balance

sheets, such as those of the Crown and private organisations, are partial and incomplete. They ignore our nation's human, intellectual, social and natural capital. Plainly, without reliable data on the nation's comprehensive wealth, as well as specific knowledge about how various policy decisions will affect particular types of capital (including, for instance, the quality and quantity of ecosystem services), there is a heightened risk of policy-makers prioritising financial and manufactured capital over other forms of capital, most notably natural capital. In so doing, they are likely to short-change the future.

But the challenges of responding to these deficiencies should not be underestimated. In particular, valuing natural capital, along with the ecosystem services it provides, poses formidable conceptual, methodological and ethical issues. Fortunately, various governments around the world, together with major international agencies like the World Bank, are devoting significant resources to such matters with the aim of building more comprehensive and rigorous accounting frameworks. We need to draw on the fruits of these labours and do our best to improve the range and quality of our data and reporting. But such activities require care: neither the intrinsic value of nature nor the worth of human beings can be fully embraced within a spreadsheet. Measures of comprehensive wealth will always be inexact and incomplete; they will only ever convey part of the story. Nevertheless, having *some* information is better than having none at all – as long as it is interpreted sensibly. Knowing whether our stocks, say, of renewable natural capital are rising or falling is important for judging whether we are genuinely getting better off or worse off, as well as assessing what the future may hold. Likewise, knowing more about the condition of our ecosystem services is crucial for prudent anticipatory governance. There is much work to be done here.

Prioritising path dependence and irreversibility
In undertaking risk assessments and analysing the merits of various policy options, it is critically important to consider the potential for substantial path dependence (e.g. due to substantial sunk costs or technological lock-ins) and/or irreversible effects. The issue of irreversibility is exceptionally important from the perspective of long-term wellbeing, yet is often overlooked or downplayed by policy advisers. When things of value are very likely to be lost forever, we need to think long and hard about whether such a loss could ever be morally justified, what future generations might conclude about our assessment and decisions, and what would be required to avoid – or greatly minimise the chances of – such a loss.

Here is a little exercise that you might like to undertake. Take a moment to go on-line and look at recent policy papers produced by government departments, especially documents dealing with major long-term issues, such as fiscal sustainability, protecting biodiversity or mitigating climate change. Then count how often they refer to 'irreversibility' or 'irreversible effects' – or perhaps impacts of a 'permanent' or 'lasting' nature. You may be surprised at how rarely such considerations are mentioned. Why is this?

Taking a precautionary approach
The idea that governments should adopt a precautionary approach in their decision-making remains controversial in some quarters. It is argued that such an approach undermines innovation and reduces economic growth. Concerns are also raised about the number of false alarms and 'false positives' – that is, the unwarranted consideration or over-regulation of minor hazards and the regulation of risks that subsequently turn out to be non-existent. Yet the available international evidence suggests that these criticisms generally lack substance.[41]

For one thing, there tend to be far more instances of 'false negatives' (i.e. cases where early warnings existed but no preventative actions were taken) than false positives. This is despite widespread endorsement in advanced democracies, including New Zealand, of some kind of precautionary principle over many years, as evidenced by its inclusion in statutory instruments. An international review several years ago of 88 cases of alleged false positives, for instance, found that, with few exceptions, they either constituted real risks or the jury was still out.[42] Altogether, there were only four clear examples of regulatory false positives.

For another, the costs of being wrong are generally asymmetrical. In other words, a failure to act on the basis of credible early warnings typically ends up costing a lot more than an excessive focus on avoiding regulatory harm. Also, while the costs of mistaken regulatory action are mainly economic and short-term, the costs of a failure to intervene are often broader and more enduring.

Within New Zealand, the precautionary approach and its implications needs to be better understood. It also needs to be applied by policy-makers and regulators more widely and consistently – ideally as part of an integrated model of risk management and an adaptive approach to governance and planning. Internationally, there are a number of well-established guidelines for the application of the precautionary principle,[43] and an appropriate version should be incorporated within New Zealand's regulatory framework.

Above all, where there are reasonable grounds for concern in the face of uncertain outcomes, the emphasis should be on avoiding or minimising harm, even at the risk of some false alarms. At the same time, policy processes must be sufficiently nimble to enable adaptive and flexible management of risks in the light of changing conditions and technologies.

6. NURTURING A FUTURE-FOCUSED POLITICAL CULTURE

If governments are to anticipate and safeguard the future, they need an active, informed citizenry who take future risks and vulnerabilities seriously and are willing to support policies involving non-simultaneous exchanges. They also need the capacity and mechanisms to negotiate durable political bargains to tackle long-term policy problems – bargains that are prudent, effective, efficient and fair, and stick long enough to make a substantive difference. In short, this means nurturing a future-focused political and intellectual culture, strengthening existing policy-making arrangements, and developing new deliberative mechanisms that can contribute to sensible cross-party agreements.

Enhancing our political institutions and policy-making processes is probably easier than changing our political culture – although the two are obviously connected. Internationally, there is a wealth of experience regarding deliberative mechanisms for conflict resolution and consensus-building, as well as a large academic literature on such matters.[44] There are many different models, with varying scales, procedures, selection criteria and participative modes. New Zealand has experimented with some of these models in recent years, such as the Land and Water Forum and the occasional citizens' jury. But we need to be bolder and braver and test a wider range of institutional mechanisms and participative processes. The possibilities here include: high-level stakeholder forums; collaborative processes; Swedish-type commissions (involving a mix of politicians, officials, academic experts and NGO representatives); and citizen-based 'mini-publics' (e.g. citizens' assemblies, citizens' juries, citizens' panels, national issues forums, consensus conferences, planning cells and deliberative polls).[45] Innovative approaches invariably run risks. There will doubtless be failures. But there is sufficient evidence of success to warrant taking some risks. Moreover, as the political theorists Robert Goodin and John Dryzek argue, initiatives that 'accord ordinary citizens a more central place in political processes' must surely be part of any strategy to 'improve democratic practice' and confront complex societal problems.[46]

On the broader question of nurturing a political culture that supports, indeed celebrates, sound anticipatory governance, the importance of political trust and shared goals cannot be underestimated. A low-trust environment is antithetical to future-focused decision-making. If people do not trust their leaders, they will afford them little slack. Likewise, if the society is characterised by significant ideological polarisation, it will be harder to reach agreement on long-term goals, let alone the policies needed to secure them. A core question, then, is how to build political trust, shared understanding and a sense of common purpose. There is no simple remedy. But the ingredients must include competent leadership, political honesty and a high level of transparency in government decision-making. There is also good evidence that egalitarian societies witness higher levels of political trust and lower polarisation than those with more unequal distributions of income and wealth.[47] Egalitarianism has other benefits too: greater social cohesion, higher rates of social mobility, and possibly higher rates of economic growth.[48] Prior to the late 1980s, New Zealand had a comparatively egalitarian distribution of income. This is no longer the case. But how might we return to a more equal society? This constitutes one of the great challenges of the twenty-first century. Whether we succeed will likely affect not only the quality of our societal relationships and the opportunities enjoyed by our citizens, but also our political capacity to safeguard our long-term interests.

IMPROVING ENVIRONMENTAL STEWARDSHIP AND ADAPTIVE GOVERNANCE

Long-term environmental interests are particularly vulnerable to short-termist decision-making, as argued in Chapter 2. The institutional reforms recommended above should contribute in various ways to protecting environmental values. But the need to improve the quality of environmental governance is urgent. It will require concerted and enduring efforts.

Amongst the many policy changes required, here are a few which deserve priority:[49]

1. implementing more demanding and comprehensive measures – across all sectors of the economy, including agriculture – to minimise negative environmental externalities (e.g. via price-based mechanisms);
2. removing environmentally damaging subsidies (e.g. for fossil fuel exploration and production);
3. providing stronger national guidance for local authorities, with more stringent biophysical bottom lines (especially for air, water and marine resources);

4. developing tighter rules to protect aggregate renewable natural capital and compensate for losses (e.g. via explicit biodiversity offsets);

5. establishing a register of all forms of natural capital that are at risk;

6. incorporating natural capital within the periodic National Infrastructure Plans, and identifying which investments in natural capital should be prioritised;

7. applying a natural capital accounting framework to the corporate sector;

8. properly funding the research and other activities required to support the long-term goal of eradicating all non-native predators within 35 years; and

9. saving a significant part of resource rentals to compensate future generations for the irreversible loss of non-renewable resources.[50]

The challenge of climate change

Without doubt, the political and policy challenges posed by climate change are unprecedented. They include:

1. providing high-quality advice to policy-makers, at both the national and sub-national levels of government, on a range of complex intergenerational issues in a context of deep uncertainty (e.g. advice about the design

and implementation of innovative and cost-effective mitigation and adaptation strategies, based on a range of analytical techniques and approaches, such as robust decision-making, dynamic adaptive policy pathways and real options analysis tools);

2. building public support for more stringent mitigation policies, some of which will involve short-term losses (e.g. for particular sectors of the economy);

3. enhancing public understanding of the adaptation challenges that various sectors and communities will face, including more severe meteorological and hydrological events, changing pest and disease vectors, more protracted droughts and rising sea levels;

4. building the capacity of communities to adapt to the impacts of climate change and reducing vulnerabilities;

5. developing new funding instruments to help address the direct costs of, and adaptive responses to, climate change, including disaster risk-reduction strategies and initiatives, enhancing resilience, and assisting those who suffer significant climate-related losses and damages; and

6. coping with greater levels of uncertainty and the need for rapid responses to changing

circumstances and demands (e.g. large numbers of refugees, substantial economic impacts from more severe droughts and floods).

Currently, various government departments, agencies and other bodies have responsibilities for aspects of climate change policy. But given the scope, scale and complexity of the challenges, the existing institutional framework is inadequate. There is a good case for at least three new institutions: a government-supported but stakeholder-led Climate Change Forum (CCF), with a mandate to build cross-sectoral understanding and support for effective and durable policies; an independent Climate Change Committee (CCC), to commission research and provide policy advice to the government; and a Crown entity in the form of a Climate Change Adaptation Fund (CCAF), complementary and supplementary to the Earthquake Commission (EQC).

Climate Change Forum

The CCF would be designed to bring together representatives from a range of sectors and stakeholder groups (including the business community, non-governmental organisations/ civil society groups, researchers, government officials, etc.). Its purpose would be to deliberate about how best to decarbonise the New Zealand economy and adapt to the impacts of climate change. It would provide an opportunity to share information and evidence, discuss feasible transition pathways for reducing emissions, build a common understanding of the challenges and opportunities, and fashion a consensus on the best policy approaches. This would include efforts to anticipate, and differentiate between, the avoidable and unavoidable impacts of climate change.

Climate Change Committee

The CCC would be modelled on the British Committee on Climate Change established under the Climate Change Act 2008.[51] It would have a legislative mandate to provide independent and authoritative advice to the government on all matters relating to climate change. It would not be a decision-making body. It would comprise up to ten high-status individuals, all of whom would have relevant scientific, policy-related or commercial expertise. Its specific tasks would include advising the government on:

- New Zealand's long-term emissions-reduction targets;
- multi-year emissions budgets;
- mitigation strategies and policies; and
- adaptation strategies and policies.

The committee would also be charged with monitoring the government's progress in meeting its mitigation commitments and targets and its adaptation goals, and reporting to Parliament. It would have its own secretariat and be independent of government departments. It would complement and supplement the responsibilities of the Parliamentary Commissioner for the Environment. Ideally, a CCC of the kind envisaged would be established in a context where the government was committed, as in Britain, to setting multi-year (e.g. five-year) emissions budgets (i.e. not just fixed-point emissions-reduction targets) covering all greenhouse gases up to four budgets ahead – i.e. looking out up to twenty years. Currently, New Zealand is some distance from securing a multi-party agreement on such a policy regime.

Climate Change Adaptation Fund

Adapting to climate change during the twenty-first century and beyond will be costly, complex and challenging – technically and politically.[52] In effect, humanity will be confronted with a slow-motion disaster that will grow progressively (but sometimes abruptly) in scale and scope, with multiple and compounding risks, and significant uncertainty. For New Zealand, much coastal infrastructure and many coastal properties will eventually be negatively affected. Hence, growing numbers of people will need to relocate from areas at risk from rising sea levels, higher water tables, and more frequent and severe flooding. But already local councils are struggling to secure public support for the required changes to zoning arrangements and planning provisions. Some opposition, of course, is understandable. After all, those directly affected face falling property values, higher insurance premiums and the eventual loss of their homes – and, in some cases – their livelihoods. From a policy perspective, a core issue is how to design institutional arrangements that can help lessen public resistance to sensible adaptive strategies and enable smoother and fairer transitions.

In this regard, the aim of the CCAF would be to complement and supplement the work of the EQC. It would have a prospective rather than retrospective mandate. Specifically, it would help to manage and fund the process of adaptation and provide compensation to those negatively affected by major climate-related impacts, especially sea level rise. Such funding would be allocated on well-defined statutory criteria which would include principles of equity, such as ability to pay, and knowledge of avoidable losses.

Like the National Disaster Fund administered by EQC and the New Zealand Superannuation Fund, the CCAF would pre-fund some of the future costs of adaptation through government-imposed levies (e.g. on household insurance and greenhouse gas emissions). Such levies could be supplemented by regional or local levies in those areas of the country which are most severely affected, probably on the basis of existing rating mechanisms.

The aim of partial pre-funding would be two-fold. First, it would enhance intergenerational justice by requiring current generations to contribute modestly towards the costs of the damage they will inflict on future generations via their greenhouse gas emissions. Second, it would provide an additional source of funds to cover some of the long-term adaptation costs facing governments and citizens.

The specific roles of the CCAF would include:

- overseeing a public fund designed to meet some of the long-term costs of adaptation, including the costs of risk-reduction strategies and preventative measures by sub-national government;
- providing compensation for the loss of private property resulting from managed retreat;
- funding research on climate change adaptation; and
- providing advice to sub-national governments and citizens on adaptation issues and options, including adaptive governance.

If well designed, the CCAF should facilitate the development of more proactive adaptation strate-

Figure 5.1 Ways of improving anticipatory governance

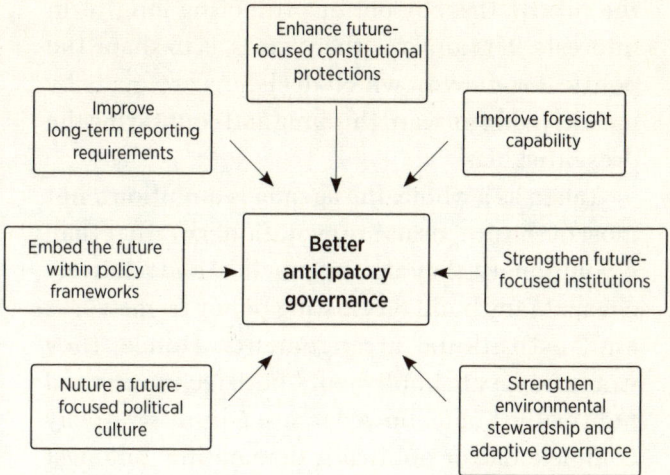

gies by local authorities, thereby reducing vulnerability and long-term damages and lowering the overall costs of adaptation. At the same time, it will be important to minimise moral hazard – that is, the possibility of people taking greater risks (e.g. in their property investments) as a result of knowing that a mechanism exists to provide (partial) compensation for climate change-related damage.

CONCLUSION

The reform agenda outlined above, and depicted in summary form in Figure 5.1, is designed to alter the decision-making environment in ways that shift the temporal focus of policy-makers towards the future, thereby better protecting long-term interests. The aim, in other words, is to shape the political *context* in which decisions are made by incentivising forward thinking and countering the presentist bias.

Taken as a whole, the agenda is ambitious. But most of the proposals are evolutionary rather than revolutionary; they are also practical and relatively cheap. Many build on existing policy frameworks and institutional arrangements. Hence, they would be easy to implement – both technically and politically. Some, however, are administratively complex and/or politically demanding. Amongst these are the proposals to develop new and more exacting measures of comprehensive wealth and reform our environmental governance, including policies to mitigate and adapt to climate change. Yet if we are serious about anticipating and safeguarding the future, we must be bold and aspirational. Too much is at stake to do otherwise.

The question of how the policy changes recommended here might be implemented is beyond the scope of this analysis. In some cases new legislation will be required or existing legislation amended. Realistically, this will only be possible with governmental support. This means persuading either the current government or a future one of the merits of the proposed reforms.

Such persuasion requires reasoned argument and vigorous advocacy. Since future generations cannot advocate on their own behalf, the responsibility falls on current citizens. In a democracy, there is no other way.

6. SAFEGUARDING THE FUTURE
OUR VISION MATTERS

… on earth, as it is in heaven … – The Lord's Prayer

Amongst the best-known prayers, certainly within the Christian tradition, is the Lord's Prayer. Strikingly, this petition to God engages both the future and the present. Strikingly, too, the concern for the future comes first: 'Your Kingdom come, Your will be done, on earth as it is in heaven.'[1] It is only after reflecting on the goal of a better life and a better world – one here 'on earth' that is more heavenly – that the prayer invokes the practical needs of the present moment: 'Give us today our daily bread …'

Is this temporal sequence accidental and inconsequential? Perhaps, but I suspect not. Having a vision of a better tomorrow is critical for living well today. It provides purpose, direction and hope.

A succinct, well-known line from Proverbs captures this truth: 'Where there is no vision, the people perish'.[2] But of course we need a deeply ethical, meaningful and inspiring vision, not any old vision. It must be ambitious, appealing and aspirational. It must facilitate new and creative thinking; motivate, captivate, empower and transform. It must generate a profound and enduring longing. Realistically, any such vision must include a recognisably better world – 'on earth as it is in heaven' – one that is more just, compassionate, humane, sustainable and life-enhancing.

Ultimately, safeguarding the future relies on citizens who care passionately about the future, yearn for a safe and rewarding prospect for future generations and are motivated to pursue their dreams. In giving expression to this quest, the virtue of anticipation constitutes an essential ingredient. Moreover, this virtue needs practical realisation not only amongst individuals, but also collectively and institutionally. At the political level, this must include a commitment to sound anticipatory governance.

As outlined in Chapter 3, such governance has many attributes. Above all, it means having governments that take care of tomorrow today. Plainly, this is a difficult task. Governments face a daunting array of risks, incessant demands, policy trade-offs, and much uncertainty – indeed, often deep uncertainty. Moreover, there is a constant risk that the urgent problems of today will divert attention from, and thwart efforts to address, the problems of tomorrow. As a result, future generations may be needlessly and unjustifiably burdened.

To mitigate such risks, governments must take countervailing measures. In particular, they need strong commitment devices that oblige policy-makers to look beyond their immediate horizons. This includes institutional mechanisms and procedural requirements that bring the long term sharply and repeatedly into short-term political focus, such as regular, dedicated and independent analyses of intergenerational issues. Governments also need, in the face of numerous unavoidable risks, to pursue strategies to enhance societal resilience and adaptive capacity. This must include, where appropriate, the adoption of 'no-regret' and 'low-regret' policies (i.e., ones that make sense across a range of plausible scenarios).

New Zealand has taken significant strides to protect future interests in recent decades, most notably in the fields of fiscal policy, public investment and public sector management, and some aspects of infrastructure planning. But in many other fields, especially social and environmental policy, the current institutional arrangements and policy frameworks are deficient.

Too often governments ignore early warnings. They fail to take prudent and timely decisions to investigate and then minimise foreseeable hazards. They neglect the importance of preserving future options. And they underinvest in evidence-based measures to reduce long-term societal costs or enhance long-term benefits. As a result, our social and ecological deficits are growing and our future liabilities are accumulating. In some cases, regrettably, the consequences will be irreversible. We have a responsibility to future generations to do better.

This book has described the nature of anticipatory governance, how it might be assessed, and how it can be incentivised, embedded and improved. The aim here is not for perfection. Such a goal is beyond our reach. But betterment is within our grasp – and critically important. The reforms outlined in Chapter 5 offer practical suggestions for securing a more sustainable and resilient future by protecting vital long-term interests – interests shared by every citizen, whether living now or in the future. It is in all our interests to take up the challenge. Safeguarding our future 'on earth' and that of future generations depends on it.

ACKNOWLEDGEMENTS

This book draws heavily on material derived from a more extensive treatment of the nature, causes, consequences and possible solutions to the 'presentist bias' (or political myopia) in democratic decision-making, published in *Governing for the Future: Designing Democratic Institutions for a Better Tomorrow* (Emerald, 2016). Numerous people contributed in various ways to the completion of that book – reviewing chapters, providing or checking data, drawing attention to relevant literature, debating ideas, and preparing tables and figures. I am enormously grateful for all this assistance.

Additionally, many people commented helpfully on earlier drafts of this BWB Text, including a much shorter analysis, 'Anticipatory Governance', published in *Policy Quarterly* (August 2016). I would particularly like to thank the following people for their assistance and advice: David Bagnall, Reid Basher, Mark Blair, Marie Brown, Ralph Chapman, Andrew Colman, Charlotte Denny, Quentin Duthie, Chris Eichbaum, Elizabeth Eppel, Derek Gill, Shaun Hendy, Peter Hughes, Andrew Jackson, Kirsten Jensen, Girol Karacaoglu, Judy Lawrence, Michael Mintrom, Toby Moore, Sir Geoffrey Palmer, Brian Perry, Murray Petrie,

Chris Purchas, Max Rashbrooke, Mike Reid, Ralph Sims, Mpaphi Tsholofelo, David Tombs, Ken Warren, Sally Washington, Iain White and Derek Woodard-Lehman.

I am also deeply indebted to Anna Hodge for her superb copy-editing and the staff of Bridget Williams Books, especially Bridget Williams and Tom Rennie, for their helpful guidance, advice and editorial oversight. Having said this, I take full responsibility for the contents of the book and, in particular, any errors of fact or erroneous interpretations of evidence.

NOTES

Chapter 1

1   Lord Martin Rees, 'If I Ruled the World', *Prospect*, 222, August 2014.

2   Surprisingly, perhaps, while there is a large literature on concepts like 'environmental governance', 'Earth-system governance' and 'intergenerational issues' (including 'intergenerational equity'), there is only a modest amount written specifically on the nature and requirements of 'intergenerational governance'.

3   For various perspectives on the concept of 'anticipatory governance' see L. Fuerth with E. Faber, *Anticipatory Governance: Practical Upgrades – Equipping the Executive Branch to Cope with Increasing Speed and Complexity of Major Challenges*, Washington, D.C., Elliott School of International Affairs, George Washington University, 2012; and L. Fuerth with E. Faber, 'Anticipatory Governance: Winning the Future', *The Futurist*, 47, 3 (July–August 2013), pp.42–49; D. Guston, 'Understanding "Anticipatory Governance"', *Social Studies of Science*, 44, 2 (March 2014), pp.218–42; R. Quay, 'Anticipatory Governance: A Tool for Climate Change Adaptation', *Journal of the American Planning Association*, 76, 4 (Autumn 2010), pp.496–511.

4   The arguments in this book draw heavily on some of my previously published work, most notably J. Boston, *Governing for the Future: Designing Democratic Institutions for a Better Tomorrow*, Emerald, Bingley, 2016; J. Boston, 'Anticipatory Governance: How Well is New Zealand Safeguarding the Future?', *Policy Quarterly*, 13, 3 (August 2016), pp.11–24; J. Boston and F. Lempp, 'Climate Change: Explaining and Solving the Mismatch between Scientific Urgency and Political Inertia', *Accounting, Auditing and Accountability Journal*, 24, 8 (2011), pp.1000–21; J. Boston and R. Prebble, 'The Role and Importance of Long-term Fiscal Planning', *Policy Quarterly*, 9, 4 (November 2013), pp.3–8; J. Boston and T. Stuart, 'Protecting the Rights

of Future Generations: Are Constitutional Mechanisms an Answer?', *Policy Quarterly*, 11, 2 (May 2015), pp.60–71; and J. Boston, J. Wanna, V. Lipski and J. Pritchard (eds), *Future-proofing the State: Managing Risks, Responding to Crises and Building Resilience*, ANU Press, Canberra, 2014.

5 There is a vast literature on this topic. See, for instance, K. Arrow, et al., 'Are We Consuming Too Much?', *Journal of Economic Perspectives*, 18, 3 (2004), pp.147–72; E. Brown Weiss, *In Fairness to Future Generations: International Law, Common Patrimony, and Intergenerational Equity*, The United Nations University, Tokyo, 1989; G. Chichilnisky, 'An Axiomatic Approach to Sustainable Development', *Social Choice and Welfare*, 13, 2 (1996), pp.231–57; A. Gosseries and L. Meyer (eds), *Intergenerational Justice*, Oxford University Press, Oxford, 2009; J. Tremmel (ed.), *Handbook of Intergenerational Justice*, Cheltenham, Edward Elgar, 2006; J. Tremmel, *A Theory of Intergenerational Justice*, Earthscan, London, 2009; World Commission on Environment and Development, *Our Common Future*, Oxford University Press, New York, 1987; S. Zuber, 'Measuring Intergenerational Fairness', in I. González-Ricoy and A. Gosseries (eds), *Institutions for Future Generations*, Oxford University Press, Oxford, 2017, pp.65–82.

6 G. Karacaoglu, *The New Zealand Treasury's Living Standards Framework: A Stylised Model*, The Treasury, Wellington, 2015.

7 Pope Francis, *Laudato Si': On Care for Our Common Home*, Encyclical Letter, The Vatican, Rome, 2015.

8 For various analyses of 'future proofing' see Boston, et al. (eds), *Future-proofing the State*.

9 N. Taleb, *The Black Swan: The Impact of the Highly Improbable*, Penguin, London, 2007.

10 Donald Rumsfeld, 2002, see 'There are known knowns', Wikipedia, https://en.wikipedia.org/wiki/There-are-known-knowns.

11 For reflections on the challenges of governing under 'deep' uncertainty, see R. Lempert, 'Creating Constituencies for Long-term, Radical Change', John Brademas Center for the Study of Congress, New York University, Research Brief

No. 2, 2007; R. Lempert, 'Can Scenarios Help Policymakers to Be Both Bold and Careful?', in F. Fukuyama (ed.), *Blindside: How to Anticipate Forcing Events and Wild Cards in Global Politics*, The Brookings Institution Press, Washington, D.C., 2007, pp.109–119; R. Lempert, S. Popper and S. Bankes, *Shaping the Next One Hundred Years: New Methods for Quantitative, Long-term Policy Analysis*, MR-1626-RPC, RAND, Santa Monica, 2003; R. Lempert and S. Popper, 'High-Performance Government in an Uncertain World', in R. Klitgaard and P. Light (eds), *High Performance Government: Structure, Leadership, and Incentives*, The RAND Corporation, Santa Monica, 2005, pp.113–136; and R. Lempert, et al. (eds), *Shaping Tomorrow Today: Near-term Steps Towards Long-term Goals*, The RAND Corporation, Santa Monica, 2009; G. Room, *Complexity, Institutions and Public Policy*, Edward Elgar, Cheltenham, 2011.

12   Lempert, Popper and Bankes, *Shaping the Next One Hundred Years*.

13   It is important to distinguish the 'presentist bias' from the literary and philosophical ideas associated with

'presentism'. See Boston, *Governing for the Future*, ch. 1.

14   For analyses of the presentist bias in democratic decision-making, see W. Ascher, *Bringing in the Future: Strategies for Farsightedness and Sustainability in Developing Countries*, Chicago University Press, Chicago, 2009; Boston, *Governing for the Future*, esp. Part 1; Boston and Lempp, 'Climate Change'; I. González-Ricoy and A. Gosseries (eds), *Institutions for Future Generations*, Oxford University Press, Oxford, 2017; A. Healy and N. Malhotra, 'Myopic Voters and Natural Disaster Policy', *American Political Science Review*, 103, 3 (2009), pp.387–406; P. Heller, *Who Will Pay? Coping with Aging Societies, Climate Change and Other Long-term Fiscal Challenges*, IMF, Washington, D.C., 2003; A. Jacobs, *Governing for the Long Term: Democracy and the Politics of Investment*, Cambridge University Press, Cambridge, 2011; A. Jacobs, 'Policymaking for the Long Term in Advanced Democracies', *Annual Review of Political Science*, 19 (June 2016), pp.433–54; A. Jacobs and J. Matthews, 'Why Do Citizens Discount the Future? Public Opinion and the Timing

of Policy Consequences', *British Journal of Political Science*, 42, 4 (October 2012), pp.903–35; Oxford Martin Commission for Future Generations, *Now for the Long Term: The Report of the Oxford Martin Commission for Future Generations*, Oxford Martin School, Oxford, 2013; D. Thompson, 'Democracy in Time: Popular Sovereignty and Temporal Representation', *Constellations*, 12, 2 (2005), pp.245–61; D. Thompson, 'Representing Future Generations: Political Presentism and Democratic Trusteeship', *Critical Review of International Social and Political Philosophy*, 13, 1 (2010), pp.17–37.

15 See, for instance, Commission for Financial Literacy and Retirement Income, *Focusing on the Future: Report to Government*, Commission for Financial Literacy and Retirement Income, Wellington, 2013; N. Kirkup, 'The Future Costs of Retirement Income Policy and Ways of Addressing Them', *Policy Quarterly*, 9, 4 (November 2013), pp.29–34; The Treasury, *He Tirohanga Mokopuna: 2016 Statement on the Long-Term Fiscal Position*, The Treasury, Wellington, 2016.

16 See, for instance, OECD, *OECD Economic Outlook: New Zealand – Overview*, OECD, Paris, June 2015, esp. pp.22–24; P. Howden-Chapman, *Home Truths: Confronting New Zealand's Housing Crisis*, Bridget Williams Books, Wellington, 2015.

17 See, for instance, I. Bailey and T.H. Jackson, 'New Zealand and Climate Change: What Are the Stakes and What Can New Zealand Do?', *Policy Quarterly*, 12, 2 (May 2016), pp.3–12; M. Brown, R. Stephens, R. Peart and B. Fedder, *Vanishing Nature: Facing New Zealand's Biodiversity Crisis*, Environmental Defence Society, Auckland, 2015; R. Chapman, *Time of Useful Consciousness: Acting Urgently on Climate Change*, Bridget Williams Books, Wellington, 2015; G. Palmer, 'Climate Change and New Zealand: Is it Doom or Can We Hope?', *Policy Quarterly*, 11, 4 (November 2015), pp.15–25; M. Joy, *Polluted Inheritance: New Zealand's Freshwater Crisis*, Bridget Williams Books, Wellington, 2015; A. Macey, 'Climate Change: Towards Policy Coherence', *Policy Quarterly*, 10, 2 (May 2014), pp.49–56; OECD, *OECD Environmental Performance Reviews: New Zealand 2007*,

Paris, OEDC, 2007; Royal Society of New Zealand, *Transition to a Low-carbon Economy for New Zealand*, Royal Society, Wellington, 2016; Royal Society of New Zealand, *Climate Change Implications for New Zealand*, Royal Society, Wellington, 2016.

18 See, for instance, Tony Blakely, 'An Open Letter to Cabinet Ministers from 74 Health Professors Calling for a Sugary Drinks Tax', 2 April 2016, https://blogs.otago.ac.nz/ pubhealthexpert/2016/04/02/ an-open-letter-to-cabinet- ministers-from-74-health- professors-calling-for-a- sugary-drinks-tax/; F. Sassi, *Obesity and the Economics of Prevention: Fit not Fat*, OECD, Paris, 2010; K. Workman, 'Back to Churchill – An Old Vision for Prisoner Reintegration', *Policy Quarterly*, 5, 2 (May 2009), pp.24–31; J. Boston and S. Chapple, *Child Poverty in New Zealand*, Bridget Williams Books, Wellington, 2014; Howden-Chapman, *Home Truths*.

19 See, for instance, New Zealand Productivity Commission, *Using Land for Housing*, Productivity Commission, Wellington, 2015, esp. pp.56–60; R. Blakeley, 'The Planning Framework for Auckland "Super City": An Insider's View', *Policy Quarterly*, 11, 4 (November 2015), pp.3–14; Jason Krupp, '… Auckland Council is Right to Give Nimbys the Finger', 30 November 2015, www.interest.co.nz/ opinion/78899/new-zealand- initiative%E2%80%99s-jason- krupp-grudgingly-argues- auckland-council-right-give.

20 New Zealand Productivity Commission, *Using Land for Housing*, esp. pp.185–91.

21 Countries differ markedly in the extent to which they save some of the proceeds of resource rentals. See, for instance, R. Murphy and J. Clemens, *Reforming Alberta's Heritage Fund: Lessons from Alaska and Norway*, The Fraser Institute/ Alberta Prosperity Initiative, Vancouver, 2013.

22 J. Key, 'Launch of Policy Project Frameworks', 23 August 2016, https:// national.org.nz/news/2016- 08-23-launch-of-policy- project-frameworks.

23 Ibid., quoting P. Varghese.

24 See, for instance, Brown, et al., *Vanishing Nature*; Intergovernmental Panel on Climate Change, *Climate Change 2013: The Physical Science Basis. Contribution of Working Group I to the*

Fifth Assessment Report of the Intergovernmental Panel on Climate Change, Cambridge University Press, Cambridge, 2013; J. Rockström, et al., 'Planetary Boundaries: Exploring the Safe Operating Space for Humanity', *Ecology and Society*, 14, 2 (2009), www.ecologyandsociety.org/vol14/iss2/art32/main.html.

25 See, for instance, D. Barton, 'Capitalism for the Long Term', *Harvard Business Review*, March 2011, https://hbr.org/2011/03/capitalism-for-the-long-term; R. Curran and A. Chapple, *Overcoming the Barriers to Long-term Thinking in Financial Markets*, Forum for the Future, Dorking, Surrey, 2011; Ernst & Young, *Short-termism in Business: Causes, Mechanics and Consequences*, EY Poland Report, Warsaw, 2014; J. Gleeson-White, *Six Capitals: The Revolution Capitalism Has to Have – Or Can Accountants Save the Planet?* Allen & Unwin, Sydney, 2014; W. Galston and E. Kamarck, 'More Builders and Fewer Traders: A Growth Strategy for the American Economy', Centre for Effective Public Management, Brookings Institution, Washington, D.C., 2015; A. Haldane, 'Patience and Finance', 9 September 2010, www.bankofengland.co.uk/archive/Documents/historicpubs/speeches/2010/speech445.pdf; A. Haldane, 'Growing, Fast and Slow', 17 February 2017, www.bankofengland.co.uk/publications/Documents/speeches/2015/speech797.pdf; J. Kay, *The Kay Review of UK Equity Markets and Long-term Decision Making*, Final Report, London, July 2012.

26 J. Guldi and D. Armitage, *The History Manifesto*, Cambridge University Press, Cambridge, 2014.

27 The concept of a 'commitment device' refers to a mechanism that is designed to change the structure of intertemporal pay-offs and/or limit future discretion by binding a person, organisation or government to a particular course of action. Commitment devices can take many different forms, from marriage vows to multiparty agreements. In the policy realm they can include constitutional or quasi-constitutional mechanisms, procedural and substantive devices, and mechanisms that are designed to insulate decisions from short-term political influence (e.g. transferring decision-rights to an independent group of experts). See, for instance,

Boston, *Governing for the Future*, esp. ch. 8; R. Reeves, 'Ulysses Goes to Washington: Political Myopia and Policy Commitment Devices', Centre for Effective Public Management, Brookings Institution, Washington, D.C., 2015.

28 See Edmund Burke, *Reflections on the Revolution in France*, James Dodsley, London, 2002 (originally published in November 1790).

29 John Rawls, *A Theory of Justice*, Harvard University Press, Cambridge, Mass., 1971, p.287.

30 Ibid., p.293.

31 Brown Weiss, *In Fairness to Future Generations*, pp.23–24.

32 See, for instance, J. Rockström, et al., 'Planetary Boundaries'; J. Rockström, et al., 'A Safe Operating Space for Humanity', *Nature*, 461, 24 (September 2009), pp.472–75.

33 The New Zealand Labour Party has been actively considering such matters in recent years. See the report of the Future of Work Commission, *The Future of Work*, Labour Party, Wellington, 2016.

34 Amongst the notable exceptions to the centralisation of policy-making in New Zealand are urban planning, resource management and environmental protection.

35 See, for instance, Barton, 'Capitalism for the Long Term'; Curran and Chapple, *Overcoming the Barriers to Long-term Thinking in Financial Markets*; Ernst & Young, *Short-termism in Business*; Haldane, 'Patience and Finance'; Kay, *The Kay Review of UK Equity Markets*.

Chapter 2

1 Al Gore, *Earth in the Balance: Ecology and The Human Spirit*, Houghton Mifflin, New York, 1992, p.170.

2 Quay, 'Anticipatory Governance', p.507.

3 World Economic Forum, *The Global Risks Report 2017*, 12th edn, World Economic Forum, Geneva, 2017.

4 R. Basher, 'High Stakes: Disaster Risk in New Zealand', *Policy Quarterly*, 12, 3 (August 2016), pp.25–29; Department of the Prime Minister and Cabinet, *National Hazardscape Report*, Officials' Committee for Domestic and External Security Coordination, Wellington, 2007; Local Government New Zealand, *Managing Natural Hazard Risk in New Zealand: Towards More Resilient Communities: A Think Piece for Local and Central*

Government and Others with a Role in Managing Natural Hazards, Local Government New Zealand, Wellington, 2014; K. Warren, 'Evidence of Resilience of New Zealand's Capitals', internal Treasury paper, Wellington, 2014.

5   See, for instance, A. Wood, I. Noy and M. Parker, 'The Canterbury Rebuild Five Years On from the Christchurch Earthquake', *Bulletin*, 79, 3 (February 2016), pp.3–16.

6   Nonetheless, governments often underinvest in such matters. See, for instance, Healy and Malhotra, 'Myopic Voters and Natural Disaster Policy'.

7   For an introduction to the literature on government failure see, for instance, J. Le Grand, 'The Theory of Government Failure', *British Journal of Political Science*, 21, 4 (October 1991), pp.423–42; C. Wolf, 'Market and Non-market Failures: Comparison and Assessment', *Journal of Public Policy*, 7, 1 (January 1987), pp.43–70.

8   For various perspectives on 'creeping problems' or 'slow-motion' problems see European Environment Agency, *Late Lessons from Early Warnings: Science, Precaution, Innovation*, European Environment Agency, Copenhagen, 2013; R. Olson, *Missing the Slow Train: How Gradual Change Undermines Public Policy and Collective Action*, Wilson Centre, Washington, D.C., 2016; V. Schneider, P. Leifeld and T. Malang, 'Coping with Creeping Catastrophes: National Political Systems and the Challenge of Slow-moving Policy Problems', in B. Siebenhner, et al. (eds), *Long-Term Governance of Social-Ecological Change*, Routledge, New York, 2013, pp. 221–38.

9   There are four main types of ecosystem services: *supporting* (e.g. soil formation, crop pollination and nutrient recycling); *provisioning* (e.g. the production of raw materials, minerals, food and water); *regulating* (e.g. waste decomposition, carbon sequestration, water and air purification, and the control of the climate system); and *cultural* (e.g. spiritual, recreational, scientific and therapeutic). See the Millennium Ecosystem Assessment, www.millenniumassessment.org/en/index.html.

10   See Boston, *Governing for the Future*, esp. chs 2 and 3; Jacobs, *Governing for the Long Term*; Olson, *Missing the Slow Train*.

11 C. Kousky, J. Pratt and R. Zeckhauser, 'Virgin Versus Experienced Risks', in E. Michel-Kerjan and P. Slovic (eds), *The Irrational Economist: Making Decisions in a Dangerous World*, Public Affairs, New York, 2010, pp.145–158.

12 E. Weber, 'Experience-based and Description-based Perceptions of Long-term Risk: Why Global Warming Does Not Scare Us (Yet)', *Climatic Change*, 77, 1-2 (2006), pp.103–20.

13 For analyses of the role of policy framing, see Ascher, *Bringing in the Future*; Jacobs, *Governing for the Long Term*.

14 See, for instance, H. Rittel and M. Webber, 'Dilemmas in a General Theory of Planning', *Policy Sciences*, 4 (1973), pp.155–69; R. Lazarus, 'Super Wicked Problems and Climate Change: Restraining the Present to Liberate the Future', *Cornell Law Review*, 94, 5 (2009), pp.1153–234.

15 See National Audit Office, *Early Action: Landscape Review*, Report by the Comptroller and Auditor General, HC 683 Session 2012–13, London, 2013.

16 Room, *Complexity, Institutions and Public Policy*.

17 See, for instance, J. Elster, *Ulysses Unbound: Studies in Rationality, Precommitment, and Constraint*, Cambridge University Press, Cambridge, 2000; J. Hovi, D. Sprinz and A. Underdal, 'Implementing Long-term Climate Policy: Time Inconsistency, Domestic Politics, International Anarchy', *Global Environmental Politics*, 9, 3 (2009), pp.20–39; F. Kyland and E. Prescott, 'Rules Rather than Discretion: The Inconsistency of Optimal Plans', *Journal of Political Economy*, 85, 3 (1977), pp.473–92.

18 For a recent analysis of the problem of securing durable political bargains and what to do about it, see O. Ilott, J. Randall, A. Bleasdale and E. Norris, *Making Policy Stick: Tackling Long-term Challenges in Government*, Institute for Government, London, 2016.

19 Jacobs and Matthews, 'Why Do Citizens Discount the Future?'

20 See, for instance, Chapman, *Time of Useful Consciousness*; R. Garnaut, *The Garnaut Climate Change Review*, Cambridge University Press, Melbourne, 2008; R. Garnaut, 'The Carbon Tax: Early Experience and Future Prospects', in D. Adamson, J. Quiggin and D. Quiggin (eds), *Carbon Pricing: Early*

Experiences and Future Prospects, Edward Elgar, Cheltenham, 2014; R. Garnaut, 'Australia after Paris: Will We Use Our Potential To Be the Energy Superpower of the Low-carbon World?', 21 January 2016, https://blogs.unimelb.edu.au/rossgarnaut/files/2015/12/Garnaut_YEP_Perth_210116v3-11wt3dw.pdf.

21 For various perspectives on such matters see Jacobs, *Governing for the Long Term*; C. James, 'Making Big Decisions for the Future', *Policy Quarterly*, 9, 4 (December 2013), pp.21–28; J. Mansbridge and C. Martin (eds), *Negotiating Agreements in Politics*, Taskforce Report, American Political Science Association, Washington, D.C., 2013.

22 Jacobs, 'Policymaking for the Long Term'; E. Patashnik, *Putting Trust in the U.S. Budget: Federal Trust Funds and the Politics of Commitment*, Cambridge University Press, New York, 2000.

23 See, for instance, S. Caney, 'Climate Change and The Future: Discounting for Time, Wealth, and Risk', *Journal of Social Philosophy*, 40, 2 (2009), pp.163–86; S. Frederick, G. Loewenstein and T. O'Donoghue, 'Time Discounting and Time Preference: A Critical Review', *Journal of Economic Literature*, 40, 2 (2002), pp.351–401; M. Spackman, 'Public Investment and Discounting in the European Union Member Countries', *OECD Journal of Budgeting*, 1, 2 (2001), pp.213–60.

24 Jacobs, *Governing for the Long Term*, 33–38.

25 A. Mani, S. Mullaninathan, E. Shafir and J. Zhao, 'Poverty Impedes Cognitive Function', *Science*, 341, (August 2013), pp.976–80.

26 C. Sunstein, *Why Nudge: The Politics of Libertarian Paternalism*, Yale University Press, New Haven, 2014, pp.36–37.

27 For a range of perspectives on such matters see Sunstein, *Why Nudge*; C. Marshall, *Compassionate Justice: An Interdisciplinary Dialogue with Two Gospel Parables on Law, Crime, and Restorative Justice*, Cascade Books, Eugene, 2012; K. Milkman, T. Rogers and M. Bazerman, 'Harnessing Our Inner Angels and Demons: What We Have Learned about Want/Should Conflicts and How that Knowledge Can Help Us Reduce Short-sighted Decision-making', *Perspectives on Psychological Science*, 3, 4 (2008), pp.324–38; J. Waldron,

'Who is My Neighbour? Humanity and Proximity', *The Monist*, 86, 3 (2002), pp.333–54.

28 See A. Bandura, 'Selective Moral Disengagement in the Exercise of Moral Agency', *Journal of Moral Education*, 31, 2 (2002), pp.101–19; A. Bandura, 'Impeding Ecological Sustainability through Selective Moral Disengagement', *International Journal of Innovation and Sustainable Development*, 2, 1 (2007), pp.8–35.

29 For accessible introductions to such matters, see D. Kahneman, *Thinking, Fast and Slow*, Macmillan, London, 2011; R. Thaler and C. Sunstein, *Nudge: Improving Decisions about Health, Wealth and Happiness*, Yale University Press, New Haven, 2008. For an analysis of how a presentist bias can affect the decision-making of individuals, especially those suffering from material deprivation, see K. Gandy, et al., *Poverty and Decision-making: How Behavioural Science Can Improve Opportunity in the UK*, The Behavioural Insights Team, London, 2016.

30 World Commission on Environment and Development, *Our Common Future*, p.8.

31 Note, too, that in most countries, publicly listed companies have fiduciary obligations to their shareholders but not to their wider stakeholders. This has significant implications for the incentives facing company directors and senior executives. See, for instance, Gleeson-White, *Six Capitals*.

32 See, for instance, Boston and Lempp, 'Climate Change'; Gleeson-White, *Six Capitals*; D. Helm, *Natural Capital: Valuing the Planet*, Yale University Press, New Haven, 2015; J. Stiglitz, A. Sen and J. Fitoussi, *Report by the Commission on the Measurement of Economic Performance and Social Progress*, Commission on the Measurement of Economic Performance and Social Progress, Paris, 2009.

33 See, for instance, M. Barber and N. McCarty, 'Causes and Consequences of Polarization', in J. Mansbridge and C. Martin (eds), *Negotiating Agreements in Politics*; J. Thurber, 'Assessing Presidential-Congressional Relations: The Need for Reform?', in J. Thurber (ed.), *Rivals for Power: Presidential-Congressional Relations*, 5th edn, Rowman & Littlefield Publishers, Lanham, 2013.

34 For instance, there is survey evidence that people are more willing to pay their taxes to fund long-term investments when they have confidence that the government will spend their taxes prudently. See Jacobs and Matthews, 'Why Do Citizens Discount the Future?'

35 See J. Boston, 'Purchasing Policy Advice: The Limits of Contracting Out', *Governance*, 7, 1 (1994), pp.1–30; M. Sako, 'The Role of "Trust" in Japanese Buyer-Supplier Relationships', *Ricerche Economiche*, 45 (1991), pp.449–74.

36 See, for instance, B. Rothstein, *Social Traps and the Problem of Trust: Theories of Institutional Design*, Cambridge University Press, Cambridge, 2005; B. Rothstein, *The Quality of Government: Corruption, Social Trust, and Inequality in International Perspective*, Chicago University Press, Chicago, 2011; B. Rothstein and E. Uslaner, 'All for All: Equality, Corruption and Social Trust', *World Politics*, 58, 1 (2005), pp.41–72; R. Wilkinson and K. Pickett, *The Spirit Level: Why Equality Is Better for Everyone*, Penguin, London, 2010.

37 Rothstein, *The Quality of Government*.

38 See Boston, *Governing for the Future*, esp. ch. 4.

39 See Boston, *Governing for the Future*, esp. ch. 4; M. Brown, et al., *Vanishing Nature*.

Chapter 3

1 J. Rawls, 'The Idea of an Overlapping Consensus', *Oxford Journal of Legal Studies*, 7, 1 (1987), p.24.

2 Fuerth and Faber, *Anticipatory Governance*, p.1.

3 For different perspectives, see Fuerth and Faber, *Anticipatory Governance*; Guston, 'Understanding "Anticipatory Governance"'; Quay, 'Anticipatory Governance'.

4 Fuerth and Faber, *Anticipatory Governance*, p.7.

5 Ibid.

6 Ibid.

7 Ibid., p.8.

8 Guston, 'Understanding "Anticipatory Governance"'.

9 See Quay, 'Anticipatory Governance', p.498.

10 See Guston, 'Understanding "Anticipatory Governance"'; and 'The Project', Project Anticipation, www. projectanticipation. org/index.php?option=com_ content&view=article&id= 3&Itemid=472.

11 There are many different versions of the precautionary principle, with widely divergent implications for

decision-making. Key issues include: when and how a precautionary approach is applied; where the burden of proof should rest for demonstrating the existence or absence of a threat of harm; how the potential threats should be balanced against other relevant considerations; and how responsibility for any harm should be allocated. See D. Gee, 'More or Less Precaution', in European Environment Agency, *Late Lessons from Early Warnings*, 2013, pp.643–69; L. Cameron, 'Environmental Risk Management in New Zealand – Is There Scope to Apply a More Generic Framework?', Policy Perspectives Paper 06/06, Treasury, Wellington, 2006; K. Foster, P. Vecchia and M. Repacholi, 'Science and the Precautionary Principle', *Science*, 288, 5468 (2000), pp.979–81; S. Gardiner, 'A Core Precautionary Principle', *The Journal of Political Philosophy*, 14, 1 (2005), pp.33–60; T. O'Riordan and A. Jordan, 'The Precautionary Principle in Contemporary Environmental Politics', *Environmental Values*, 4, 3 (1995), pp.191–212.

12   'Black elephants' are a combination of black swan events and the proverbial 'elephants in the room'.

Hence, they are problems which everyone is aware of but which people pretend are not there because they don't want to deal with them. See Peter Ho, 'Society at Risk: Hunting Black Swans and Taming Black Elephants', 5 December 2016, www.csf.gov.sg/docs/default-source/default-document-library/2016-12-05-peter-ho---society-at-risk.pdf, pp.4–5.

13   See J. Lawrence, 'The Implications of Climate Change for New Zealand's Natural Hazard Risk Management', *Policy Quarterly*, 12, 3 (August 2016), pp.30–39.

14   Ibid.

15   See H. Aaron, 'Presidential Address: Seeing through the Fog: Policymaking with Uncertain Forecasts', *Journal of Policy Analysis and Management*, 19, 2 (2000), pp.193–206.

16   The concept of resilience is increasingly central to many policy debates. But it is also a contested concept. For several views on the nature and utility of the concept, see F. Brand and K. Jax, 'Focusing the Meaning(s) of Resilience: Resilience as a Descriptive Concept and a Boundary Object', *Ecology and Society*, 12, 1 (2007), p.23; S. Davoudi, 'Resilience, a

Bridging Concept or a Dead End?', *Planning Theory and Practice*, 12, 2 (2012), pp.299–307; O'Hare, I. White and A. Connelly, 'Insurance as Maladaptation: Resilience and the "Business as Usual" Paradox', *Environment and Planning C: Government and Policy*, 34, 6 (September 2016), pp.1175–193.

17 Warren, 'Evidence of Resilience'.

18 World Economic Forum, *Global Risks 2013*, 8th edn, World Economic Forum, Geneva, 2013, pp.38–39.

19 See United Nations International Strategy for Disaster Reduction Secretariat, *Risk and Poverty in a Changing Climate: 2009 Global Assessment Report on Disaster Risk Reduction*, United Nations, New York, 2009.

20 For various contributions to the subject, see K. Arrow, et al., 'Sustainability and the Measurement of Wealth', *Environment and Development Economics*, 3, 17 (2012), pp.317–53; K. Bosselmann, *The Principle of Sustainability: Transforming Law and Governance*, Ashgate, Aldershot, 2008; K. Hamilton and J. Hartwick, 'Wealth and Sustainability', *Oxford Review of Economic Policy*, 30 (2014),

pp.170–87; Helm, *Natural Capital*; World Commission on Environment and Development, *Our Common Future*.

21 There is an extensive literature on deliberative democracy. See, for instance, J. Dryzek, *Deliberative Democracy and Beyond*, Oxford University Press, Oxford, 2000; J. Dryzek, *Deliberative Global Politics: Discourse and Democracy in a Divided World*, Polity Press, Cambridge, 2006; J. Fishkin and P. Laslett (eds), *Debating Deliberative Democracy*, Blackwell Publishing Press, Oxford, 2003.

22 For various perspectives on 'good' governance see Rothstein, *The Quality of Government*; F. Fukuyama, 'What is Governance?', *Governance*, 26, 3 (2013), pp.347–68; R. Gregory, 'Assessing "Good Governance": "Scientific" Measurement and Political Discourse', *Policy Quarterly*, 10, 1 (February, 2014), pp.15–25.

23 See, for instance, Ascher, *Bringing in the Future*; Boston, *Governing for the Future*; Boston and Prebble, 'The Role and Importance of Long-term Fiscal Planning'; González-Ricoy and Gosseries, *Institutions for*

Future Generations; Jacobs, *Governing for the Long Term*; James, 'Making Big Decisions for the Future'; Mansbridge and Martin, *Negotiating Agreements in Politics*; T. McLeod, 'Governance and Decision-making for Future Generations: Background Paper', Oxford Martin Commission on Future Generations, Oxford Martin School, Oxford, 2013; E. Ostrom, 'Beyond Markets and States: Polycentric Governance of Complex Economic Systems', Nobel Prize lecture, Workshop in Political Theory and Policy Analysis, Indiana University, Bloomington, 2009; Reeves, 'Ulysses Goes to Washington'.

Chapter 4

1   See Boston and Prebble, 'The Role and Importance of Long-term Fiscal Planning', and other articles in the same issue of the journal. For the details of the 2013 Statement, see The Treasury, *Affording our Future: Statement on New Zealand's Long-Term Fiscal Position*, The Treasury, Wellington, 2013. For the details of the 2016 Statement, see The Treasury, *He Tirohanga Mokopuna*.

2   See Public Finance Act 1989, S26N(2)(b)(i).

3   See The Treasury, *He Tirohanga Mokopuna*.

4   See Public Finance Act, S26NA(2). See also The Treasury, *Investment Statement: Managing the Crown's Balance Sheet*, The Treasury, Wellington, 2014.

5   Standing Orders 2014, 336(1) (d) and (e).

6   See, for instance, Controller and Auditor-General, *Water and Roads: Funding and Management Challenges*, Office of the Controller and Auditor-General, Wellington, 2014.

7   For the first synthesis report see Ministry for the Environment and Statistics New Zealand, *Environment Aotearoa 2013 – Data to 2013*, Wellington, 2015. See also: Parliamentary Commissioner for the Environment, *The State of New Zealand's Environment: Commentary by the Parliamentary Commissioner for the Environment on 'Environment Aotearoa 2015'*, Parliamentary Commissioner for the Environment, Wellington, 2016.

8   See, for instance, Judy Lawrence, 'The Adequacy of Institutional Frameworks and Practice for Climate Change Adaptation Decision Making', Ph.D. thesis, Victoria University of Wellington, Wellington, 2015.

9   Warren, 'Evidence of Resilience'.

10 Transparency International New Zealand, *Integrity Plus 2013: New Zealand National Integrity System Assessment*, Transparency International New Zealand, Wellington, 2013.

11 These requirements were incorporated into the Public Finance Act 1989 in 2004.

12 New Zealand Government, *New Zealand Coastal Policy Statement 2010*, Department of Conservation, Wellington, 2010.

13 J. Ayto, 'Why Departments Need To Be Regulatory Stewards', *Policy Quarterly*, 10, 4 (November 2014), pp.23–27.

14 For some international examples and perspectives see J. Leach and A. Hanton, *Intergenerational Fairness Index 2015*, Intergenerational Foundation, London, 2015; Zuber, 'Measuring Intergenerational Fairness'.

15 For instance, Section 10(c) of the Fisheries Act 1996 requires decision-makers to 'be cautious when information is uncertain, unreliable, or inadequate', while Section 7 of the Hazardous Substances and New Organisms Act 1996 require a 'precautionary approach' to be applied by all those 'exercising functions, powers, and duties' under the Act.

16 For an analysis of the precautionary principle and its application in New Zealand see Cameron, 'Environmental Risk Management in New Zealand'. See also Office of the Prime Minister's Chief Science Advisor, *Making Decisions in the Face of Uncertainty: Understanding Risk, Part 1*, Office of the Prime Minister's Chief Science Advisor, Wellington, 2016.

17 Ibid.

18 See Marie Brown and Jemma Penelope, 'Biodiversity Offsets in New Zealand: Addressing the Risks and Maximising the Benefits', *Policy Quarterly*, 12, 1 (February 2016), pp.35–41.

19 See Helm, *Natural Capital*, esp. pp.55–75.

20 See, for instance, Policy 27(2)(B) of the New Zealand Coastal Policy Statement 2010.

21 The most recent National Infrastructure Plan was published in 2015. National Infrastructure Unit, 'The Thirty Year New Zealand Infrastructure Plan 2015', The Treasury, www.infrastructure.govt.nz/plan/2015/nip-aug15.pdf.

22 See Parliamentary Commissioner for the Environment, *Preparing New Zealand for Rising Seas:*

Certainty and Uncertainty, Parliamentary Commissioner for the Environment, Wellington, 2015.

23 See Lawrence, 'The Implications of Climate Change for New Zealand's Natural Hazard Risk Management'.

24 For an analysis of the adaptation issues facing New Zealand, see M. Manning et al., 'Dealing with Changing Risks: A New Zealand Perspective on Climate Change Adaptation', *Regional Environmental Change*, 15, 4 (April 2015), pp.581–94.

25 See Boston, *Governing for the Future*, esp. ch. 12.

26 For an introduction to the Treasury's Living Standards Framework, see B. Gleisner, M. Llewellyn-Fowler and F. McAlister, 'Broadening our Understanding of Living Standards: Treasury's New Policy Framework', *Policy Quarterly*, 7, 3 (August 2011), pp.13–19. For an overview of the Natural Resources Framework see E. Hearnshaw, et al., 'Stewardship and the Natural Resources Framework', *Policy Quarterly*, 10, 1 (February 2010), pp.35–44. See also Gabriel Makhlouf, 'Growing Our Economic Capital: Investing in Sustainable Improvement in Our Wellbeing', 3 November 2016, www.treasury.govt.nz/publications/media-speeches/speeches/growing-economic-capital/sp-economiccapital-3nov16.pdf.

27 See 'The Role of the Chief Science Advisor', Office of the Prime Minister's Chief Science Advisor, www.pmcsa.org.nz/the-role-of-the-chief-scientific-advisor/; 'Briefing Note: The New Zealand Science Advisory System', Office of the Prime Minister's Chief Science Advisor, www.pmcsa.org.nz/wp-content/uploads/Overview-of-NZ-science-advisory-system.pdf.

28 See Ayto, 'Why Departments Need To Be Regulatory Stewards'.

29 For details of the Better Public Services initiative see 'Better Public Services', State Services Commission, www.ssc.govt.nz/better-public-services

30 See Royal Society of New Zealand Act 1997, S6.

31 For an assessment of the Parliamentary Commissioner for the Environment, see, for instance, T. Bührs, 'Barking Up Which Trees? The Role of New Zealand's Parliamentary Watchdog', *Political Science*, 48, 1 (1996), pp.1–28; D. Young, *Keeper of the Long View*, Parliamentary Commissioner for the Environment,

Wellington, 2007.

32 See Ministry of Social Development, *The Social Report 2016 – Te Pūrongo Oranga Tangata*, Ministry of Social Development, Wellington, 2016.

33 See, for instance, the critique of *Environment Aotearoa 2015* by the Parliamentary Commissioner for the Environment, *The State of New Zealand's Environment*.

34 See Basher, 'High Stakes: Disaster Risk in New Zealand'; Lawrence, 'The Implications of Climate Change for New Zealand's Natural Hazard Risk Management'.

35 Basher, 'High Stakes: Disaster Risk in New Zealand'.

36 See, for instance, R. Blakeley, *Building Community Resilience*, SOLGM, Wellington, 2016.

37 See Basher, 'High Stakes: Disaster Risk in New Zealand'.

38 At the time of writing, such a register was in preparation.

39 For details see S. St John, 'Superannuation: Where Angels Fear to Tread', in J. Boston, P. Dalziel and S. St John (eds), *Redesigning the Welfare State in New Zealand: Problems, Policies, Prospects*, Oxford University Press, Auckland, 1999, pp.278–98.

40 C. Martin, 'Negotiating Political Agreements', in J. Mansbridge and C. Martin (eds), *Negotiating Agreements in Politics*; C. Martin, 'Conditions for Successful Negotiation: Lessons from Europe', in J. Mansbridge and C. Martin (eds), *Negotiating Agreements in Politics*.

41 Ibid.; James, 'Making Big Decisions for the Future'.

42 For an analysis of the Land and Water Forum see E. Eppel, 'Collaborative Governance Case Studies: The Land and Water Forum', Working Paper No. 13/05, Institute for Governance and Policy Studies, Victoria University of Wellington, Wellington, 2013.

43 See Parliamentary Commissioner for the Environment, *The State of New Zealand's Environment*, p.27.

44 For instance, under the current restoration plan of the Waikato Regional Council, it is estimated that it will take up to eighty years to restore the ecological health of New Zealand's longest river, the Waikato, and its major tributary, the Waipa, so that they will be safe for gathering food and swimming. See Environment Waikato, *Healthy Rivers: Plan for Change/Wai Ora: He Rautaki Whakapaipai*, 2016.

45 For recent assessments see

The Treasury, *He Tirohanga Mokopuna*; Ministry of Social Development, *The Social Report 2016*.

46 Ministry of Health, *Annual Update of Key Results 2014/15: New Zealand Health Survey*, Ministry of Health, Wellington, 2015; 'Annual Update of Key Results 2014/15: New Zealand Health Survey', Ministry of Health, www.health.govt.nz/publication/annual-update-key-results-2014-15-new-zealand-health-survey; 'Facts and Figures', Smokefree, www.smokefree.org.nz/smoking-its-effects/facts-figures.

47 See 'The Social Report 2016 – Te pūrongo oranga tangata', Ministry of Social Development, http://socialreport.msd.govt.nz/health/potentially-hazardous-drinking.html.

48 R. Buckle and A. Cruikshank, 'The Requirements for Long-run Fiscal Sustainability', Working Paper 13/20, The Treasury, Wellington, 2013; N. Gemmell and D. Gill, 'The Myth of the Shrinking State? What Does the Data Show about the Size of the State in New Zealand 1900–2015', *Policy Quarterly*, 12, 3 (August 2016), pp.3–10.

49 See Boston and Chapple, *Child Poverty in New Zealand*, esp.

chs 1 and 2.

50 See UNICEF Office of Research, *Fairness for Children: A League Table of Inequality in Child Well-being in Rich Countries*, Innocenti Report Card 13, UNICEF Office of Research, Florence, 2016; Boston and Chapple, *Child Poverty in New Zealand*, esp. ch. 10; and Education Counts, www.educationcounts.govt.nz/home.

51 See Ministry of Health, *Annual Update of Key Results 2014/15*.

52 See Howden-Chapman, *Home Truths*; Boston and Chapple, *Child Poverty in New Zealand*, esp. ch. 9.

53 See M. Adams and R. Chapman, 'Do Denser Urban Areas Save on Infrastructure? Evidence from New Zealand's Territorial Authorities', *Policy Quarterly*, 12, 4 (November 2016), pp.63–70.

54 See Auckland Council, *Getting Auckland Moving: Alternative Funding for Transport Discussion Document*, 2012; R. Blakeley, 'The Planning Framework for Auckland "Super City": An Insider's View'.

55 See Brown, et al., *Vanishing Nature*; Chapman, *Time of Useful Consciousness*; Joy, *Polluted Inheritance*; Macey, 'Climate Change:

Towards Policy Coherence';
OECD, *OECD Environmental
Performance Reviews*.

56 See Brown, et al., *Vanishing
Nature*; Warren, 'Evidence of
Resilience of New Zealand's
Capitals'.

57 Ministry for the Environment
and Statistics New Zealand,
*Our Marine Environment 2016:
Data to 2015*, Ministry for the
Environment and Statistics
New Zealand, Wellington,
2016, p.7.

58 Parliamentary Commissioner
for the Environment, *The State
of New Zealand's Environment*,
p.18.

59 See D. Hicks, et al., 'Suspended
Sediment Yields from New
Zealand Rivers', *Journal
of Hydrology*, 50 (2011),
pp.81–142.

60 See Chapman, *Time of
Useful Consciousness*; Macey,
'Climate Change: Towards
Policy Coherence'.

61 See Pieter Vanhuysse,
'Measuring Intergenerational
Justice – Towards a Synthetic
Index for OECD Countries',
in *Intergenerational Justice
for Aging Societies: A Cross-
national Comparison of 29
OECD Countries*, Bertelsmann
Stiftung, Gütersloh, 2013,
pp.10–43.

62 Ibid.

63 The establishment of the NZ
Superannuation Fund in the
early 2000s is significant in
this regard. In 2016 its assets
exceeded \$31 billion.

Chapter 5

1   J. McGlade, 'Preface', in
European Environment
Agency, *Late Lessons from
Early Warnings*, p.8.

2   S. Hansen and J. Tickner,
'The Precautionary Principle
and False Alarms – Lessons
Learned', in European
Environment Agency, *Late
Lessons from Early Warnings*,
p.12.

3   See Boston, *Governing for the
Future*, Part 3.

4   Parliamentary Commissioner
for the Environment, *The State
of New Zealand's Environment*,
p.24.

5   G. Palmer and A. Butler, *A
Constitution for Aotearoa New
Zealand*, Victoria University
Press, Wellington, 2016, p.13.

6   Ibid.

7   See Boston, *Governing for
the Future*, ch. 7. Currently,
of over 190 lower houses
and unicameral national
legislatures, only 10 have a
term of three years or less,
75 have a four-year term, and
103 have a five-year term.
See 'Parliaments at a glance',
Inter-Parliamentary Union,
www.ipu.org/parline-e/
ParliamentsAtaGlance.asp.

8   See J. Boston, *Governing Under*

Proportional Representation, Institute for Policy Studies, Wellington, 1998, pp.114–17.

9   See, for instance, G. Brennan and J. Buchanan, *The Reason of Rules: Constitutional Political Economy*, Cambridge University Press, New York, 1985.

10 Antonio Rangel, 'Forward and Backward Intergenerational Goods: Why is Social Security Good for the Environment?', *American Economic Review*, 93, 3 (2003), pp.813–34.

11 See Transparency International New Zealand, *Integrity Plus 2013*. See also Murray Petrie, 'Building and Maintaining Trust in Public Institutions: Is This Possible?', in Boston et al. (eds), *Future-proofing the State*, pp.87–99.

12 See, for instance, G. Miller, 'Above Politics: Credible Commitment and Efficiency in the Design of Public Agencies', *Journal of Public Administration Research and Theory*, 10, 2 (2000), pp.289–327; Reeves, 'Ulysses Goes to Washington'; T. Rogers and M. Bazerman, 'Future Lock-in: Future Implementation Increases Selection of "Should" Choices', *Organizational Behaviour and Human Decision Processes*, 106, 1 (2008), pp.1–20; T. Rogers, K. Milkman and K.

Volpp, 'Commitment Devices: Using Initiatives to Change Behaviour', *Journal of the American Medical Association*, 311, 20 (2014), pp.2065–66; J. Rutter and W. Knighton, *Legislated Policy Targets: Commitment Device, Political Gesture or Constitutional Outrage?* Institute for Government, London, 2012.

13 There are various possible ways of wording such a provision. See *Governing for the Future*, ch. 7; Palmer and Butler, *A Constitution for Aotearoa New Zealand*, p.69.

14 See Boston and Stuart, 'Protecting the Rights of Future Generations'.

15 See Parliamentary Commissioner for the Environment, *The State of New Zealand's Environment*, p.24.

16 Ibid., pp.6, 24, 45.

17 See J. Boston, S. St John and B. Stephens, 'The Quest for Social Responsibility', *Social Policy Journal of New Zealand*, 7 (December 1996), pp.2–16.

18 For instance, such analyses could consider whether there is a pro-elder bias in social expenditures. For various discussions on such matters, see Vanhuysse, 'Measuring International Justice'; P. van Parijs, 'The Disenfranchisement of the

Elderly, and Other Attempts to Secure Intergenerational Justice', *Philosophy and Public Affairs*, 27, 4 (1998), pp.292–333.

19 See Boston, et al., 'The Quest for Social Responsibility'.

20 In Finland, for instance, there is a requirement for governments to produce a report on the future every parliamentary term, but the precise requirements in relation to these reports are not specified. See Boston, *Governing for the Future*, ch. 12.

21 There are obligations in various international agreements for governments to report on progress with respect to their commitments.

22 See Boston, *Governing for the Future*, ch. 12.

23 See, for instance, Leach and Hanton, *Intergenerational Fairness Index 2015*. Note that attempts to develop a single integrated index raise major analytical and ethical challenges, not least the problem of incommensurability.

24 See Macey, 'Climate Change: Towards Policy Coherence'; R. Chapman, et al., 'Gazetting New Zealand's 2050 Emissions Target', submission to the Ministry for the Environment, Wellington, 2011.

25 For an analysis of some of the risks associated with setting targets, see C. Hood, 'Gaming in Targetworld: The Targets Approach to Managing British Public Services', *Public Administration Review*, 66, 4 (2006), pp.515–21.

26 The Future of Work Commission established by the Labour party in 2014 is a notable exception.

27 See Government Office for Science, www.gov.uk/government/organisations/government-office-for-science.

28 See Boston, *Governing for the Future*, ch. 12.

29 For details see 'About Scotland's Futures Forum', Scotland's Futures Forum, www.scotlandfutureforum.org/index.php?id=55.

30 Key, 'Launch of Policy Project Frameworks'.

31 For an assessment of the provision of free and frank advice, see Transparency International New Zealand, *Integrity Plus 2013*.

32 For details see 'Policy Project', Department of the Prime Minister and Cabinet, www.dpmc.govt.nz/policyproject. See also a blog in October 2016 by Sally Washington, who led the Policy Project: Sally Washington, 'New Zealand's reforms to improve

policymaking', 5 October 2016, www.instituteforgovernment.org.uk/blog/new-zealands-reforms-improve-policymaking.

33 S. Hendy, *Silencing Science*, Bridget Williams Books, Wellington, 2016.

34 Ibid., p.110. See also S. Hendy, 'Science for Policy: The Need for a Commission for Science', *Policy Quarterly*, 12, 3 (August 2016), pp.46–49.

35 For details see 'Current Discount Rates', The Treasury, www.treasury.govt.nz/publications/guidance/planning/costbenefitanalysis/currentdiscountrates.

36 HM Treasury, *The Green Book: Appraisal and Evaluation in Central Government*, HM Treasury, London, 2011.

37 See M. Weitzman, 'Why the Far-distant Future Should Be Discounted at Its Lowest Possible Rate', *Journal of Environmental Economics and Management*, 36 (1998), pp.201–8.

38 See 'The Treasury's CBAx Tool', The Treasury, www.treasury.govt.nz/publications/guidance/planning/costbenefitanalysis/cbax.

39 See, for instance, J. Kwakkel, W. Walker and M. Haasnoot, 'Coping with Wickedness of Public Policy Problems: Approaches for Decision-Making under Deep Uncertainty', *Journal of Water Resources Planning and Management*, 142, 3 (March 2016), pp.1–5; Lempert, Popper and Bankes, *Shaping the Next One Hundred Years*.

40 See Arrow, et al., 'Sustainability and the Measurement of Wealth'; K. Hamilton, 'Biodiversity and National Accounting', in D. Helm and C. Hepburn (eds), *Nature in the Balance: The Economics of Biodiversity*, Oxford University Press, Oxford, 2014; Hamilton and Hartwick, 'Wealth and Sustainability'; K. Hamilton and C. Hepburn, 'Wealth', *Oxford Review of Economic Policy*, 30, 1 (2014), pp.1–20.

41 See Hansen and Tickner, 'The Precautionary Principle and False Alarms'.

42 Ibid.

43 See Cameron, 'Environmental Risk Management in New Zealand'; E. Fisher, J. Jones and R. von Schomberg (eds), *Implementing the Precautionary Principle: Perspectives and Prospects*, Edward Elgar, Cheltenham, 2006.

44 James, 'Making Big Decisions for the Future'; Mansbridge and Martin, *Negotiating Agreements in Politics*.

45 See, for instance, R. Goodin

and J. Dryzek, 'Deliberative Impacts: The Macro-Political Uptake of Mini-publics', *Politics and Society*, 34, 2 (2006), pp.219–44; G. Smith, 'Deliberative Democracy and Mini-publics', in B. Geissel and K. Newton (eds), *Evaluating Democratic Innovations: Curing the Democratic Malaise?* Routledge, Abingdon, 2012.

46 Goodin and Dryzek, 'Deliberative Impacts', pp.238–39.

47 See Rothstein and Uslaner, 'All for All'; Wilkinson and Pickett, *The Spirit Level*.

48 See, for instance, A. Atkinson, *Inequality: What Can Be Done?* Harvard University Press, Cambridge, Mass., 2015; OECD, *Divided We Stand: Why Inequality Keeps Rising*, OECD, Paris, 2011; OECD, *Inclusive Green Growth for the Future We Want*, OECD, Paris, 2012; OECD, 'Trends in Income Inequality and Its Impact On Economic Growth', OECD Social, Employment and Migration Working Papers No. 163, 2014; M. Rashbrooke (ed.), *Inequality: A New Zealand Crisis*, Bridget Williams Books, Wellington, 2013; J. Stiglitz, *The Price of Inequality*, Allen Lane, London, 2012; J. Stiglitz, *The Great Divide: Unequal Societies and What We Can Do About Them*, W. W. Norton and Co., New York, 2015.

49 This list draws on suggestions from a range of sources. See, in particular, the publications of the Parliamentary Commissioner for the Environment: 'Publications', Parliamentary Commissioner for the Environment, www.pce.parliament.nz/publications; see also Brown et al., *Vanishing Nature*, pp.137–73.

50 See, for instance, the reports of the Natural Capital Committee in Britain: Natural Capital Committee (NCC), www.gov.uk/government/groups/natural-capital-committee.

51 See Committee on Climate Change, www.theccc.org.uk/. Note that in April 2016 the Parliamentary Commissioner for the Environment suggested establishing an independent climate change agency in New Zealand, possibly modelled on the British committee, in a submission on the Emissions Trading Scheme Review 2015/16. See "Emissions Trading Scheme Review 2015/16: Other Matters', Parliamentary Commissioner for the Environment, www.pce.parliament.nz/media/1658/ets-review-submission-other-

mattersfinal3.pdf.

52 See, for instance, Intergovernmental Panel on Climate Change, *Climate Change 2014: Impacts, Adaptation and Vulnerability. Contribution of Working Group II to the Fifth Assessment Report of the Intergovernmental Panel on Climate Change*, Cambridge University Press, Cambridge, 2014; Parliamentary Commissioner for the Environment, *Preparing New Zealand for Rising Seas*; Royal Society of New Zealand, *Climate Change Implications for New Zealand.*

Chapter 6

1   Matthew 6: 9–13, English Standard Version. Note that the idea of a 'kingdom' in the New Testament is not so much a physical place but rather as state of affairs characterised by the reign of God's peace and justice.

2   Proverbs 29: 18, King James Version.

ABOUT THE AUTHOR

Jonathan Boston is Professor of Public Policy in the School of Government at Victoria University of Wellington. Professor Boston is a leading contributor to policy debate in New Zealand on a range of issues. He served on the Tertiary Education Advisory Commission in 2000–01 and was the co-chair of the Children's Commissioner's Expert Advisory Group on Solutions to Child Poverty in 2012–13. The author of numerous books and articles, he contributed to *Inequality: A New Zealand Crisis* (BWB, 2013), and chaired the book's advisory group. He subsequently co-authored *Child Poverty in New Zealand* (BWB, 2014), with Simon Chapple. In 2014 he was awarded a Fulbright Fellowship to investigate ways of mitigating the 'presentist bias' in democratic governance – often referred to as 'political myopia' or 'short-termism'. A major book based on this research – *Governing for the Future: Designing Democratic Institutions for a Better Tomorrow* – was published by Emerald in late 2016.

About BWB Texts

BWB Texts are short books on big subjects: succinct narratives spanning history, memoir, contemporary issues, science and more from great New Zealand writers. All BWB Texts are available digitally, with selected works also in paperback. New Texts are published monthly – please visit www.bwb.co.nz to see the latest releases.

BWB Texts include:

Paul Callaghan: Luminous Moments
Foreword by Catherine Callaghan

Creeks and Kitchens: A Childhood Memoir
Maurice Gee

Report from Christchurch
Rebecca Macfie

Hidden Agendas: What We Need to Know about the TPPA
Jane Kelsey

Geering and God, 1965–71: The Heresy Trial that Divided New Zealand
Lloyd Geering

Inequality and the West
Robert Wade

The Zealandia Drowning Debate: Did New Zealand Sink Beneath the Waves?
Hamish Campbell

The Quiet War on Asylum
Tracey Barnett

What Happened at Waitangi?
Claudia Orange

When the Tour Came to Auckland
Geoff Chapple

Thorndon: Wellington and Home, My Katherine Mansfield Project
Kirsty Gunn

First Contact: Tasman's Arrival in Taitapu, 1642
Anne Salmond

Wellbeing Economics: Future Directions for New Zealand
Paul Dalziel & Caroline Saunders

Growing Apart: Regional Prosperity in New Zealand
Shamubeel Eaqub